HEROES

WOMEN IN SNOWBOARDING

ACC ART BOOKS

Photography

Jérôme Tanon

Words

Mary Walsh, Nirvana Ortanez, Desiree Melancon, Robin Van Gyn, Naima Antolin, Elena Graglia, Melissa Riitano, Marie-France Roy, Leila Iwabuchi, Leanne Pelosi, Anna Gasser, Mia Brookes, Annie Boulanger, Ylfa Rúnarsdóttir, Hana Beaman, Natacha Rottier, Alexis Roland, Zoë Vernon, Estelle Pensiero, Ivika Jürgenson, Klaudia Medlova, Elena Könz, Christy Prior, Crystal Legoffe, Marion Haerty, Sina Candrian, Laurie Blouin, Jamie Anderson, Zoi Sadowski-Synott, Jessa Gilbert, Yuka Fujimori, Jérôme Tanon.

Illustrations & Artworks

Tina Jeler, Natasza Zurek, Cristal Legoffe, Hannah Eddy, Sarah King, Natacha Rottier, Elena Graglia, Desiree Melancon, Jessa Gilbert, Alicia Gilmour, Christina "Pika" Burtner, Morgan Anderson, Zoë Vernon, Kaisa Lemley, Margot Rozies, Elena Könz.

Graphic Design

Matt Georges

Additional making-of photography

Julien Perly, David Malacrida

Proofreading

Sophie & Theo Acworth

Locations

Helisnki, Finland

Absolut Park, Flachauwinkl, Austria

Audi Nines, Obergurgl, Austria

Laax, Switzerland

Whistler BC, Canada

Nelson BC, Canada

Baldface Lodge, Canada

Ms. Superpark, Eldora CO, USA

Salt Lake City UT, USA

Quebec City, Canada

Chamonix, France

Estelle Pensiero & Robin Van Gyn

Morgan Anderson, *Heroes II*
Digital illustration

ARTIST STATEMENT

Women riders have always been teenage heroes to me, independent and bad-ass girls, skating, surfing, snowboarding. Despite this, in the twelve years that I have been a snowboard photographer, I have barely shot any proper epic photos of women. I didn't try hard enough. Back then girls were generally considered good for lifestyles and catalogues and boys for action ads. This, thankfully, is now changing. However, in the art of snowboard photography, there is still a lack of global photo work on women. I needed to make this project happen to partly fill this void, and to capture and illustrate the culture and progression of women in snowboarding.

I spent most of the 2019 and 2020 winters travelling to just a fraction of the numerous dedicated female snowboarders, documenting their lives in the streets, the backcountry and the snowparks. The more I shot and listened to their stories, the more I realised how vivid their love for snowboarding is, and how important this is. I am ever thankful to the riders who have welcomed me into their homes, and into the intimacy of their sessions. These colourful encounters opened my eyes and revived my own personal flame.

The photos are taken with the Pentax 6x7 medium format film camera, in black and white. In the central body of work, I etch, scratch and paint onto the precious negatives before making gelatin silver prints in the darkroom with an obscure process called lith printing. In the hope of creating timeless icons, I etched their words onto their photos.

As much as it is mine, this book also belongs to them. Alongside my photographs, they have filled these pages with their stories and works of art. This book is a declaration of love, a physical testament to women in snowboarding, to their their unique talent and total dedication.

Jérôme Tanon

Jeff Pensiero, Estelle Pensiero & Robin Van Gyn

P R E F A C E

· 🦵 · 🍕 · 🚡 · 👓 · 🎒 · 📷 ·

by Mary Walsh

Snowboarding is in the moments, the beats that occur in between turns and tricks. The subtleties of challenge and triumph that draw us in, season after season. Snowboarding is ambivalent to our obsession with it, dictated instead by the uneven rise and fall of mercury and the inconsistency of storm patterns. But still it grips us and summons us to freezing cities where we pile into vans and drive up and down streets looking for stairsets; calls us to remote, snow-covered peaks in search of untouched zones; begs us always back to the lift lines, the park laps, and the stormy days where we tear downhill with snow-plastered faces.

It is in all of these places that we collect the moments that further cement our obsession. A deep breath before an untouched line. An overnight drive for the spoils of a storm. Spots that work. Spots that don't. Spots that take try after try after try. A mid-bootpack break, breathless amidst the scenery and cursing the distance left to the top. Coffee. Lots of coffee. Shovels stuffed in boardbags, stuck into trunks, and scraped over and over against the concrete. Crowded hotel rooms. Part-time jobs. Broken bones and torn ligaments that shatter our seasons and stop our hearts — even if temporarily. The feeling of fear and the ability to keep pushing forward. Road trips and plane rides and places where you arrive knowing no one, and leave with a crew. The removal of boots, finally indoors, after hours spent outside. Wine. Lots of wine. Clips logged, lines taken, sleep deprived, lessons learned. Bonds formed over early mornings in the mountains. Late nights in the streets. Stories that fill the seconds in between the shots in a video part. That fill weeks on the road. The times when exhaustion and elation are one and the same. The welding of each winter.

If there is a common theme that runs throughout snowboarding, it is the devotion of oneself to these moments. The ups and downs, the rigors and rewards of every season. Everyone who applies themselves to this particular craft is likely filled with a lot of passion and a little lunacy. And snowboarding is better for it. If there is a driving force that runs through women's snowboarding, it is the effort of this dedication. The effort that every turn requires, that every video clip mandates, that every contract and photo and opportunity demand, in order to even exist. The consistent going above and beyond of what is expected. This has always been true for the women in snowboarding. And because of this, their grit and tenacity feed off one another to create opportunity where at times, there has been far from enough.

Jérôme Tanon's *Heroes* is a testament to this enduring women's enterprise; an ode to the current groundswell of skilled and creative female snowboarders that have renounced compliments that start and end with 'rides like a guy'. In my own experience, growing up and snowboarding in New England in the early aughts, that sentiment was tantamount to success. A decade later, when I moved to California to work as a writer and photographer in the industry at a greater scale, it was still the case. As part of the *SNOWBOARDER Magazine* staff for the better part of the past decade, I have had the unique opportunity to work on the periphery of the pursuits of my more authentically gifted peers, whether shooting photos, conducting interviews, piecing together editorial, or just acting as a sounding board. In this time, particularly in the past few years, there has been an exciting and palpable shift in the way female snowboarders are perceived, by themselves and others. Through their riding, their writing, their art, their videos, and their photography, women have made their presence known in an ever-growing renaissance of talent, the ranks of professional and amateur feeding off of one another, propelling each other forward, and forcing the rest of snowboarding to take notice. Female riders aren't just a binary of their male counterparts, a role to fill on a team roster or a model to display in a catalogue. They are, in greater numbers than ever before, a current pushing snowboarding in a direction that they see fit. Built on the kindling of the female professionals that have come before them, the present crop of women in snowboarding is stoking the fire brighter and brighter by the season, affecting the overarching industry and community as a whole. 'Women's snowboarding' is not a lesser-than designation, it is in addition to – a distinct club that all women can be a part of while still representing and greatly affecting 'snowboarding' overall.

The timing couldn't have been more ideal for *Heroes*. Two years ago, when Jérôme Tanon embarked to on this endeavour he was compelled to do so out of what he saw as necessity; he had been a professional photographer shooting snowboarding for twelve years, but had shot with few women. Looking around, he saw many accomplished female riders, but a disproportionate lack of photos. So, he set out to collaborate with women from around the world in order to document their stake in snowboarding.

What Jérôme has created in the following 288 pages is an honest portrait of the women in snowboarding, both as individuals and as they contribute to the whole. For two seasons, he worked to tell the story of the contemporary state of snowboarding in the backcountry, the streets, and the terrain park through the women at the forefront of these arenas. Of course, he found devotion; the pure love of riding bleeds through each page of *Heroes*. Every photo possesses an organic, intimate glimpse into how the subjects spend their winters, nuanced in a way that is nearly impossible to achieve in action spreads or social media posts. Jérôme has captured moments of effort, perseverance, and fulfillment – themes that are further emphasised by essays and art created by the featured athletes and other influential female snowboarders, and interspersed throughout the book. In their words, the riders lay their stories bare; personal entries of substance abuse, self-acceptance, body image, and finding oneself are intertwined with the lines left in the snow in both veteran and nascent careers. Paired with Jérôme's photos, the riders' work reinforces a shared and distinctly female experience rooted in the mountains: snowboarding can be a catalyst of change, a place of solace, a motivator, a mindfuck — though always a conduit for discovery, growth, and ultimately, acceptance. The pages of this book present a point of view that is unrefined and honest, a labour of love by everyone involved, and further enhanced by the specific techniques that Jérôme chose in bringing *Heroes* to light.

It is clear throughout all of Jérôme's work that the process is just as vital as the final result. He has a gift for discerning quietly impactful moments and working seamlessly with his subjects, and in order to do so, chooses his medium as carefully as his composition. For *Heroes*, Jérôme strayed from the DSLR cameras that are de rigueur in sports photography — cameras that offer hundreds of attempts to capture the right moments per memory card and endless opportunities for digital post-processing. Instead, Jérôme chose a purist, and at times, more punishing approach for *Heroes* that would allow him to further curate his conceptualisation. He shot the main body of work on a medium format Pentax 6x7 camera with a fixed lens, manual focus, and ten photos per roll of film. Each depression of the shutter had to be considered, each opportunity taken. Film is not inexpensive and when shooting action, less than a second can make a major difference in getting the right frame of a trick. Jérôme's choice of camera made his method more parallel to the work of the riders. For them, every attempt on a handrail is always as pivotal as the one before it. With camera-imposed limitations, Jérôme had to navigate the same knife's edge of success. Jérôme's self-awareness and ability to provide commentary on both subject, process, and artist has long been a major part of his work, and in choosing to shoot *Heroes* in this way, he acknowledges an element of absurdity to this self-imposed challenge. But isn't that a bit of what snowboarding, at its core, is about? A dedication to something seemingly frivolous but completely expressive, a joy found in the struggle toward the end result, a love of something that is filled with bruises, busts, let-downs, breakdowns, and the solidarity that those around you understand too.

That they are standing next to you, looking at the same snow, excited at all the possibility.

In the darkroom, Jérôme has employed a technique called lith printing, which is complex and a challenge to control, but pays dividends in producing high contrast images. Lith printing is more than a means to an end when developing photos, but instead is a process that allows the photographer's aesthetic and ability in the darkroom to take a greater role within the finished image. In Jérôme's case, printing each photograph was a make-or-break undertaking: he etched into meticulously collected negatives to further enhance the themes he wanted to explore, then utilised paper for the prints that is no longer in production and of which he had no extra supplies. There were no test papers. No re-dos. Each photo was given one chance at life, each moment one opportunity to tell its story.

Because of this, each photograph that Jérôme has created is steeped in the effort of snowboarding — of women's snowboarding. Every image is a recognition of the individual contributions that the women featured in *Heroes* have made to this community.

As a creator, Jérôme's auteur approach is at once hands-on in process and hands-off in observation, a style that enhances the voice of the subject via the photographer's presentation without any superfluous noise. In *Heroes*, Jérôme exposes the female side of snowboard culture with a thoughtful, considered perspective. This collection of work — a moment in snowboarding — is as much a testament to Jérôme's skill as an artist as it is to his egalitarian approach to creating that art: his photos, the riders' words, the artists' works, are bound together in this homage to the ways that women are shaping snowboarding. In *Heroes*, Jérôme showcases the contrasts in experience, style, terrain, and personality that are propelling snowboarding forward and ties them together through those very moments that drew each individual to this endeavour in the first place.

Kaisa Lemley, *Feeding Eachother*
Acrylic Ink , 11x14"

Ylfa Rúnarsdóttir, Siv Knudsen, Elena Graglia,
Sara Sakkinen, Ivika Jürgenson & Alieke Hoi

Nirvana Ortanez

Robin Van Gyn

MFR

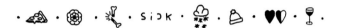

My parents separated when I was nine years old and my father became a single dad with three kids. He wanted to start skiing again and introduce us to the local mountain in Quebec so he gave us a deal to make it work. He said our Christmas gift every year would be a season's pass if we agreed to help around the house (cooking, cleaning, laundry, firewood etc.) and to get summer jobs to help pay for our gear. We were in and our lives changed. In the winter, we were on the hill every weekend, first chair to last chair every day. As the youngest with two older brothers, I just wanted to fit in and keep up so bad. And I sucked so bad too. Their crew of friends ripped and they didn't want their younger sister tagging along but my dad forced them to have me. So I never said a word and just followed. I was so committed to keeping up that sometimes I would even pee my pants while riding because I didn't want to stop and make them wait. They probably wouldn't have waited... Sometimes my brother's friends would have spitting contests on my board on the chairlift to see who could get the gnarliest biggest one to freeze on there. But as mean as it sounds, that was so much fun and I wouldn't have traded it with anything. We loved snowboarding and I loved them.

I am so grateful that my dad had my back and that my brothers let me tag along and taught me so much. I am not sure where I would be today if it wasn't for having them and snowboarding as strong influences in my life. But I sure feel like those were some of the best teachings I could have had. About love, determination, self-esteem, fear, kindness, friendship, sacrifice, about family, about how hard it must have been for our mum to have to leave, about acceptance, compassion, health and what truly brings happiness.

Marie-France Roy

Alicia Gilmour, *The VEDA*
Photo transfer on wood, 34.5" x 17.5"
Photo Zoya Lynch

Crystal Legoffe

Marie-France Roy, Leanne Pelosi & Robin Van Gyn

CL

I grew up in Whitehorse, Yukon. It's a beautiful place with an extremely dry climate, few people and a reputation for gold. My uncle worked in the ONLY board store, he got me the kind of board you pulled kids around on when they're toddlers, and then he disappeared. After that I didn't snowboard much for the next twelve years.

I was a lazy kid who disliked physical exercise; not much held my interest outside my trampoline, video games, and drawing. I grew up in a trailer 30km outside of the city with no public transit, many nights I'd help my mum clean buildings just so I didn't have to be home. My parents had a turbulent and sometimes violent relationship. They are good people that bring out the worst in each other. As I grew older fights with my alcoholic father escalated, I was angry all the time. I struggled with body image and relationships with my peers. During this time I was subject to bullying online and in person, by girls I had previously trusted. They would pull me out of class to threaten me, tell anyone I tried to connect with that I was bad news and I would ruin their lives. I felt alienated, useless, lost and depressed. I was on the verge of taking my own life.

While I was going through this personal crisis I involved myself with a group of younger boys; we beat each other up, played video games and went to our gymnastics centre. They encouraged me to try new things and showed me how great sport could be. I started going to Mt. Sima to snowboard with them. I could barely toe side carve but I would follow them anywhere on the mountain even if it was well above my skill level. The more I went snowboarding, the more confidence I gained in my self on and off the resort. I entered a boarder-cross race at our closing weekend, and I podiumed. I felt like a new person and wanted to invest in my future.

That year Snowboard Yukon held Canada Games tryouts so I decided I should learn how to hit a rail. Four girls came to tryouts, and I was selected for slopestyle. After that I moved to Whistler, where I was presented with so many opportunities to travel and meet many talented, supportive, creative men and women through sport. I've been able to create a positive narrative for myself and experienced so much happiness because of those opportunities.

I have not had a great relationship with other women most of my life, but the women in the industry have shown me it doesn't have to be like that. No matter where you go in the world you can connect with people through board sports and create a new family of friends. Without snowboarding I may have never left my small town and would probably be unhappy, or have fallen into a pattern of substance abuse to cope with my feelings. I am very grateful to be part of a community that has cultivated so much growth in my life. Thank you snowboarding.

Crystal Legoffe

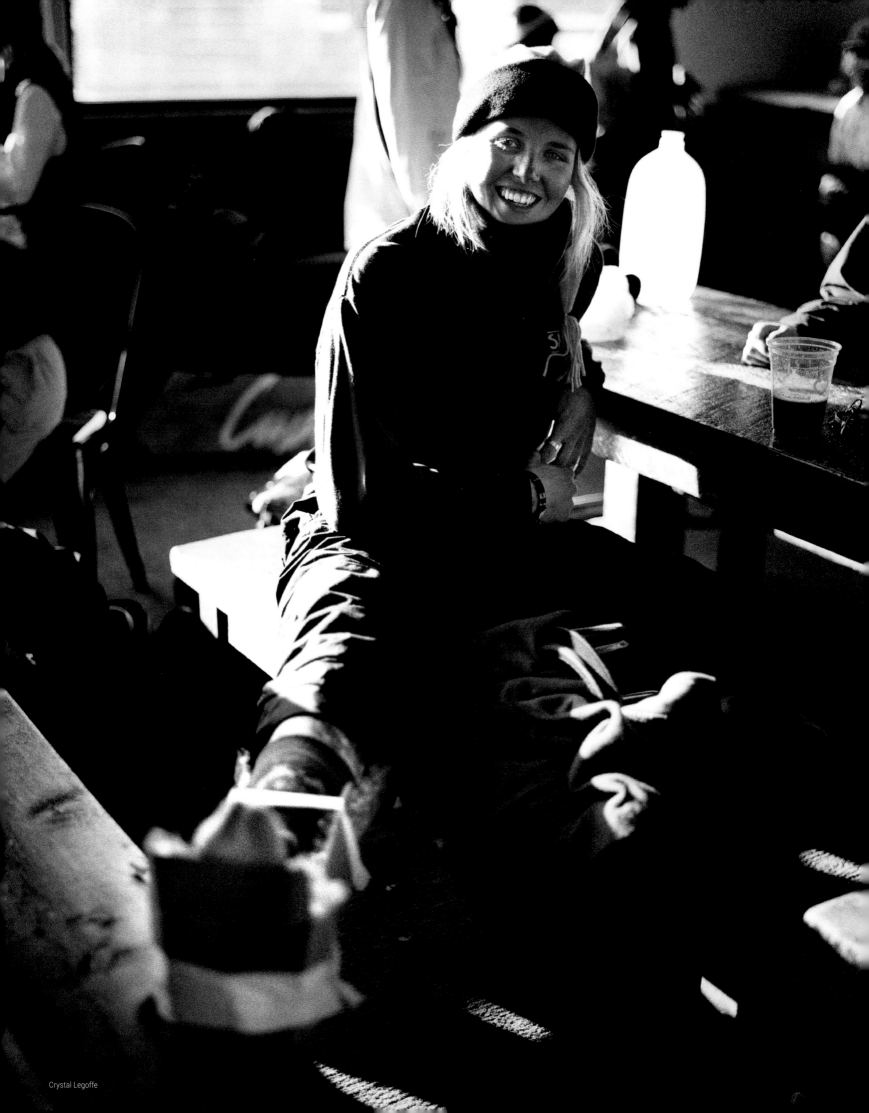

Estelle Pensiero

a n e w   p e r

spective

Laurie Blouin

c o m m

Crystal Legoffe, *Commentary*
Ink on paper, digital

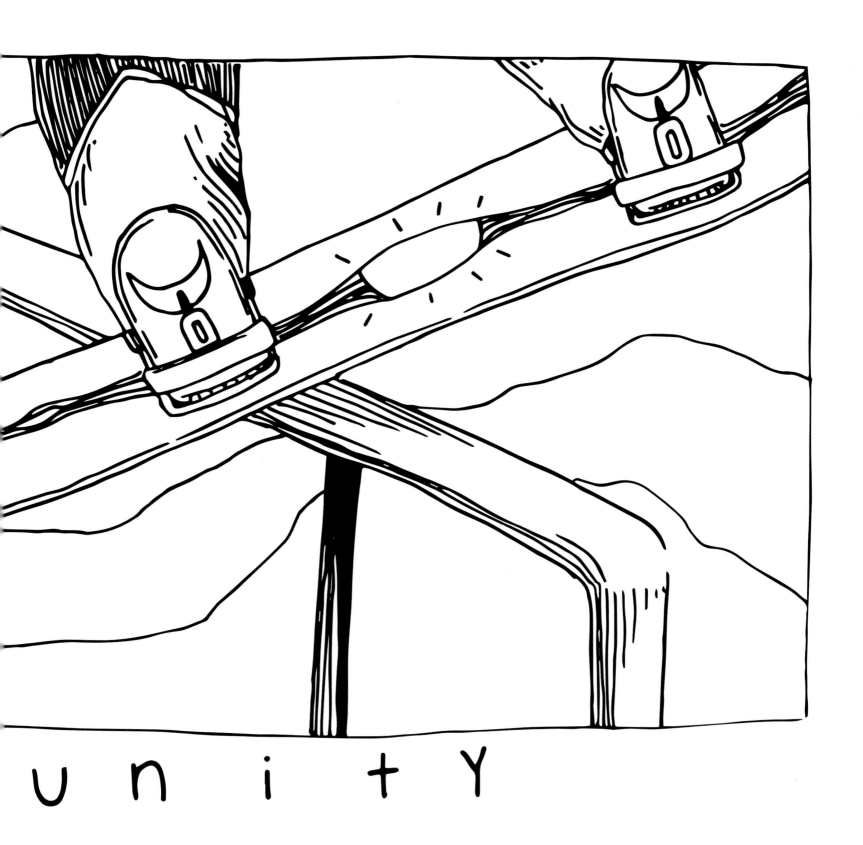

un i t Y

IJ

I live and breathe snowboarding. It has been a big part of my life ever since I turned 16. Basically, any decision I made in my life – like going to university, getting a job, where to go for a vacation, etc. – I've made by first thinking about snowboarding and then accommodating the rest of my life around it. But whatever I put aside for snowboarding, life always seems to find a way to prevent me from doing the one thing I truly want.

I'm originally from Estonia, which meant that to be able to snowboard I had to travel. We don't have any mountains, so I started snowboarding at a DIY snow park behind our school on a 10m high hill. After I graduated I knew I needed to build the rest of my life around snowboarding. But because of the culture among my friends and family, I started to feel the pressure to go to university. I'm a perfectionist, and I didn't accept anything less than A grades. It was nearly impossible to divide my time in between the 'social norm' and snowboarding so I kept torturing myself at school. That is when I decided to go to Bear Mountain and Mammoth for three months. This place changed me, I saw a lot of like-minded people and it made me more confident towards my goals in snowboarding. I didn't feel like the outsider, I was at home. I grew more confident to follow my own path in snowboarding. I finished university so I was able to do what I always wanted to: film a part.

In order to film, I need people around me. But being from Estonia turns out to be another roadblock. I didn't know anybody at the start, so I ended up contacting anybody I could think of. Being a girl doesn't help either, because it still seems most guys aren't too excited to have a random chick join on their trips. After every trip ends, I am hit with the uncertainty of whether I'll be able to join a different crew. Sometimes I end up stranded on the other side of the world, alone, waiting for the next opportunity to present itself. The desire to go snowboarding, and the uncertainty if I'll be able to, is mentally super challenging.

I spend my summers working, trying to make enough money to make it through the wintertime. Time that I feel I should be spending on the glaciers. I lost contact with most of my friends from home, I don't get to see my family nearly as much as I'd want to, and all that in the hopes of going on trips as an outsider.

These days I feel lucky to be able to go film with the Postland guys, and I have sponsors that support me throughout the winter. I feel especially grateful for everything that Tim has done for me; without him I would not have been able to film *HONEY*. Some of the clips were solo missions with just the two of us. Over the past years, he had a big influence on my snowboarding and given me the confidence to ride bigger spots and get better shots. I'm so thankful to have him in my life.

Now I've decided to change my life around and move to the mountains, so that even in-between trips I can just go snowboarding. Because when all of these challenges have been faced and I get to strap in, everything fades into the background and I'm reminded why I go through all this.

Ivika Jürgenson

Hannah Eddy, *Huck It*
Digital Illustration

Hannah Eddy, *Carve Through the Chaos*
Digital Illustration

LI

I didn't like snowboarding when I started because my father was pushy and screaming at me. It wasn't fun.

But, after I was able to think about snowboarding by myself, it felt exciting to snowboard.

I've been doing this for a long time and I can't imagine that I don't snowboard.

This is really important for me. I need this in my life. I don't even know the reasons myself.

Leila Iwabuchi

EP

I started skiing when I was a baby and spent a ton of time up at Baldface lodge, living in this little cabin called the baby barn. It was such an amazing childhood because I got to grow up surrounded by people who were inspiring me to do all sorts of things.

When I started snowboarding I was about five years old and I hated it. I always have problems with getting really upset when I try new things and am not immediately great at them. But my dad still took me out all the time and after a while, it all clicked. I stopped being frustrated that I wasn't a prodigy and was just enjoying where I was at. Then snowboarding became really fun. When I was eight my dad sent me out alone for the first time in the snowcat for the day and then I knew that snowboarding was what I wanted to do. The girls from Full Moon came up to film and I came along. Riding with all these badass women made me realise 'Oh, this is a real thing, women in snowboarding, maybe I could do that too'. And I saw how much these girls were dedicated to pushing the sport for women. I was so inspired, I wanted to be a pro literally because I had so much fun on that trip. I decided that I wanted to be a professional snowboarder and inspire other girls to go out to find their passion no matter what other people tell them.

Since I was a little kid I always had a passion for the outdoors and a curiosity for the world around me. Surrounded by these awesome mountains, they were the obvious focus for my explorations. I went all around the Baldface tenure with my dad and checked out all the bike trails, waterfalls and forests that I could get to from my house; but it wasn't until I was around 9 that I took some overnight trips in the backcountry and got into some gnarlier, less accessible mountain ranges. I realised that my joy comes directly from the mountains and from the feeling of being in the presence of these things that are so much bigger than you. The mountains don't care, they just exist, people come and go but the mountains are always there. It's just so badass! I honestly can't articulate why I am so fascinated with them but I know that when I am in the mountains I feel at home, clear-minded and happy. Snowboarding is the perfect avenue for me to explore big mountains and I know that it's what I want to do, because even though it sounds like a cliché and cheesy, I feel free from all my issues and really, really happy as soon as I drop in.

Estelle Pensiero

Jeff & Estelle Pensiero

Estelle Pensiero

Robin Van Gyn

Sarah King, *Marie at Sunset*
Pen and ink

MH

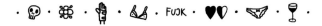

My addiction to the mountains was formed through snowboarding. A simple sunrise, a night in a refuge, a fresh breeze on my face, a snowflake on my jacket, the sound of silence and this feeling of freedom when you become one with 'Her', the mountain. Believe me, though, it was not always like this.

I had a sweet childhood growing up near Grenoble, but this quickly turned into a struggle. At the age of ten, I was thrown into adulthood when I saw the bailifs threaten to kick us out of our home. My parents and siblings were working countless hours to save the family carpentry business, and my dad was working to the point of total exhaustion. We were living in the constant stress of bank loans instead of spending time together and I was growing angry and resentful from facing the unfairness of this world around me.

After being given a board for Christmas, snowboarding became my escape. I dreamt of being a world champion one day, maybe because I wanted to help my family overcome this infernal cycle, but I also wanted to dedicate my life to a work which I would always love. So at 14, I started babysitting to pay for my snowboard camps at Chamrousse and for my first competitions. Due to lack of money, I was not able to join the school sports programme of the ski federation. This hurt, but I just kept snowboarding more and more. Thanks to my sponsors, extra jobs and friends giving me bits of advice in the snowpark, I became National Slopestyle Champion at eighteen, and I later tried for the Olympic adventure of Sochi but I wasn't able to qualify.

A few years later I recieved a wildcard invitation for the Freeride World Tour and this was the major turning point in my life. I was finally able to accomplish my childhood dreams; one year later I became World Champion and it felt like the beginning of something new. It was not just about collecting trophies for my shelf, I found the power deep inside to understand myself and know who I am. I blew off my lack of self-confidence and my shyness to draw my own way, my own line. You will think I'm crazy, but this anger inside me was so strong that it drove me to win my first world title, and I was actually scared I wouldn't be able to win again if my anger had gone!

I transitioned further from the parks to the alpine surroundings and moved to Chamonix, where I discovered a landscape beautiful and deadly all at once, filled with history, where there is so much to learn just to get to the slopes. This learning process taught me to be humble when looking at these giants of ice and rock, and to progressively try it myself. Thanks to snowboarding, I have found a way to extinguish my anger with a board under my feet, and to find peace.

Marion Haerty

Natasza Zurek, *Beauty and the Beast*
Acrylic, casein, oil on panel

Anna Gasser

Robin Van Gyn

Annika Morgan

Marie-France Roy

ZV

Snowboarding. Describing what it means to me feels like too big a task, too much to encompass with words. How it's changed my life as a whole, how the nuances have changed my day to day; my actions, my decisions. How it's broadened my world beyond belief. The people that have been brought into my life; the influences, friends, mentors, the egotists, the fame-hungry, those in it for the wrong reasons as well as those in it for the soul. The places snowboarding has taken me. Different resorts, mountains, mountain ranges, states, countries. At times it seems to have shrunken my world, kept me from pursuing a career, moving to another place, dating outside of the bubble.

Sometimes I feel like Peter Pan, stuck with the lost boys and girls in a Neverland where we eternally play and refuse to grow up. Sometimes I feel like the luckiest person alive. Who am I to be able to stand in these mountains, surrounded by breathtaking beauty, feeling no worries or anxiety, only gratitude and joy. All I know is what snowboarding makes me feel. It makes me feel every emotion on the spectrum, at one time or another. It's crazy that such a vast range of emotions all derive from this one simple thing. It makes me feel alive. Makes me feel like I'm doing something worthwhile with my time and with my life. It makes me feel like I will never look back and feel regret for the decisions I've made; to centre my life around snowboarding and shred as much as possible.

Life may change, my path may veer down a different course, who's to say. All I know is that every minute I spend snowboarding now is the best way I know how to live.

Zoë Vernon

This is how you see yourself

Zoë Vernon, *This is how you see yourself*
Pencil

Robin Van Gyn

Ylfa Rúnarsdóttir

YR

Snowboarding has been a part of my life for around ten years now. I still remember so well that feeling of freedom at the beginning of it all. Kind of like I found myself even though I wasn't really looking for anything. Then for a few years, I got caught up in insecurities and self doubt. Feeling like I was a fraud. Like I was trying too hard to fit in what my idea of a 'cool snowboarder' was. People's comments and opinions mattered too much to me and that feeling of freedom got lost.

I think I am happy that I went through that and realised what was happening. It helped me figure out the things I love about snowboarding and why I love it so much. I'm now staying true to myself and working on getting back to that feeling of freedom. Snowboarding means more to me now than ever. I snowboard for my soul and try not to get too caught up in my ego about my own snowboarding.

Ylfa Rúnarsdóttir

Tina Jeler, *Broken bones*
Hand writing

KEN
MES

CP

Pre-snowboarding, I was always into sports but nothing that gave me a real reason to put it above all else and give it everything. At the time, I had three petty crime charges, compulsory changes in schools and was rubbing shoulders with some unsavoury characters, getting involved in drugs and alcohol.

I found snowboarding at the age of seventeen and it changed everything. Yeah, we still partied, lived on couches, and worked dead-end jobs – but it was different. There was an underlying sense of purpose and it set my soul on fire. I wasn't sure where I was going but I sure as hell was enjoying the ride.

It wasn't until I saw some of my peers start to get support from sponsors and national teams, the kind of support I could only dream of while washing dishes and cleaning toilets just to keep the dream alive, that I decided to re-align my priorities. Sacrifices were made but it didn't matter. I wasn't sure it was possible but I had nothing to lose. To be honest, contests weren't my first choice but if there was a chance I could snowboard more, it was worth a try.

I set out for Breckenridge, CO, on my own in 2011, lived on a mezzanine with three others, worked under the table, and learnt how to hit jumps... The following year, an ultimatum from the NZ team led me to put all my eggs in one basket. That was when I pulled out the credit card and put it all on the line in the hope I would get a slopestyle result worthy enough to be put on the team. If it worked – great. If it didn't – debt could be worked off and at least I'd know I'd tried. That was the start of a very eventful, challenging but meaningful journey and one that I am so thankful I had the courage to follow my heart for.

Christy Prior

Broken bones:

Dislocated left shoulder, subluxed right shoulder, ruptured left shoulder ligament – didn't get it fixed, micro fracture surgery undertaken on left knee from a ruptured articular cartilage lesion, left meniscus, 30+ concussions – still rehabbing the effects of these, left bone bruising in tibia plateau, shattered both collarbones – a couple of years apart, fractured right ankle, slipped disk in back, along with sprains, strains and bruises all over.

Christy Prior

My name is Jamie Lou, I'm 29 years young and I'm fortunate to have been able to spend the last half of my life dedicated to following my passions of snowboarding and travelling the world. I'm from a little town called Meyers, near South Lake Tahoe. I'm the fifth of eight kids – five sisters and two brothers.

My dad's from Cali and absolutely loves the mountains and exploring. My mum is from Vermont, she is passionate about farming and raised our family very organically and holistically. We were home-schooled and we spent most of our time being outside in the mountains, having fun, having the freedom to be kids and be ourselves! I feel so fortunate and grateful to have grown up in the mountains with a centred, and down-to-earth adventurous family. My sisters and I always had each other's back! They inspired me to start snowboarding and pushed me to pursue professional riding. My sister Joan and I went to our first X Games together when I was 13 and she was 17. Four years later we both won gold, me in park and her in boardercross. It was a very memorable moment in my upbringing, and my whole family was there to celebrate!

For sure it hasn't always been easy, I've had my highs and my lows. Sometimes growing up, I would push so hard and have injuries and I just wanted to fucking give up. Some of the bails I've had have left me feeling so discouraged. What am I doing?! I value my health and well-being so much, why would I risk it?! We have to send it and push through our fears. I'm scared all the time. I hate being hurt, I am terrified of doing double corks and learning new tricks. But I am addicted to progression and seeing what I'm capable of. There is nothing like landing a new trick you've been thinking of for ever!

I feel life has always had my back. I have so much appreciation for all I've been able to do, and I'm excited for what's to come! I never want to stop learning. I want to give back and find more ways to help inspire the youth to love life to the fullest and most important, lead through example with gratitude and a positive attitude. We are all capable of anything we believe. Trust, believe and achieve whatever you want. I had the privilege of shooting with lots of girl crews over the years, it always inspired me, and made me so stoked to be a woman in a male-dominated sport. I looked up to Barrett Christy, Janna Meyan, Victoria Jealouse and Tara Dakides... Leanne Pelosi was a huge mentor of mine; I went to whistler at 16 to film for *Runway* and Hana Beaman doubled me up into the backcountry. I got to ride with amazing girls like MFR, Robin Van Gyn, Elena Hight, Helen Schettini. It inspired me to ride more backcountry and to connect with like-minded, strong, passionate women. Thank you snowboarding. All the women in this book are my heroes.

Jamie Anderson

Elena Graglia

HEROES

YF

I was training hard, aiming for the 2010 Olympics in snowboard cross while also shooting freestyle videos. As I became stronger in snowboard cross, pressure increased for me to concentrate on one thing and one thing only – the Olympics, which meant I had less time and freedom to shoot freestyle.

I began to feel very sad that I could not do what I liked. So I asked myself, what do I really want to do?

I realised that what I wanted to be was not just a snowboard cross racer, but to have time to freely express myself through snowboarding. When I was 28 years old, I made the decision to stop snowboard cross and to commit to freestyle snowboarding against the advice of those around me. This was hard, especially as by that age it was considered 'late' for a change of discipline, but I did not want to have any regrets in my life. I wanted to be truly passionate about what I was doing. I am proud of my decision at that time.

That one decision made my life better.

Yuka Fujimori

Desiree Melancon

Marie-France Roy

Desiree Melancon

Desiree Melancon

Tina Jeler, *Fuck*
Digital illustration

DM

My life before snowboarding provides little room for comment, aside from moments that helped develop a thick skin and a willingness for adaptation. Growing up in suburban Southern California I lived out a quintessential case of middle child syndrome in a loving family, minus an older brother who kicked the shit out of me. Constantly perceiving my female existence to be burdensome while struggling with the early onset of anxiety and depression, I numbly drifted across social climates, simultaneously exploring extrovert and introvert. Skirting across the loss of adolescence, mentally avoiding my teenage years, I eventually accumulated into an impressively rebellious mess. Adulthood abruptly took me by surprise. It was not the shock of ageing, it was the weight of manifesting a reality that I was in charge of, proud of, and not eager to depart from. Determined by the motivation that there wasn't a point in doing anything other than what I wanted, I find confidence in saying **my life didn't start until I found snowboarding.**

Throughout the years of obsessively searching for whatever it was that I was looking for, between video parts and anecdotal accolades, there was always an underlying infatuation recognised in **the feeling**. Digested in the forms of casual to late-night conversations, brainstorming, filming, hiking, following, drinking, shovelling, sweating, bleeding, carving, laughing, pandering, driving, travelling, impulsiveness, impromptu yelling matches – you name it, we have done it. Memorable moments while existing. I needed to hear and see how other people feel and felt, as a way to validate myself. Hindsight would be more useful in the moment, and in this instance there's a beauty in my revelations. It's easy to be distracted by the wonders of strapping in, an endless list describing minute moments noted through endorphins circulating analgesic effects. It is difficult for some to understand that this relief is tenuous due to the passing of sessions and seasons. While my appreciation for what snowboarding has provided remains constant, this is not without sacrifice. Opportunities were fabricated, pursued, and forced upon an industry that was bothered by my rhetoric and put off by my gender, reminding me of those same internal qualms of the feminine mystique. Credit card debt was acquired while contracts were promised then taken away, only to hopefully return again. Clip after clip filmed. Oftentimes being told it wasn't enough, other times proving 'them' wrong. Oftentimes telling myself I wasn't enough, then proving myself wrong. My body broke over and over, stitched back together by sutures and a willingness to avoid obsoletion. Every injury was a self-death and then a rebirth. I fought and fight for the underdogs, believe in the beauty of filming, and refuse to monetise my body as a means to succeed.

I am indebted and privileged to have acquired the benefits of a culture and community connected by the notion of independence, fun, freedom, and expression. Like most baby boomer offspring, I was told to pursue happiness, that I could do anything and be anyone. I proudly labelled myself a snowboarder, sealing my fate to never reap the allotted benefits of the doctors or lawyers or entertainers constituting the upper echelon of American society. Forever to spend my nights unknowing what the next day would provide. Happy. Snowboarding became more than my label but rather a tool and because of this I became an artist, an entrepreneur, a producer, a world traveller, a film-maker, a photographer, a poet, a journalist, a graphic designer, a businesswoman, a student, an activist, a raconteur, and a mentor. Without snowboarding, I am none of the above and for that I am eternally grateful.

Desiree Melancon

Pat Bridges, Desiree Melancon,
Justin Leveille, Mia Lambson

Welcome
All Visitors
Please Sign
in at Office
♿ Entrance on
Lower Level

Desiree Melancon

Naima Antolin

NA

I had a thought when I was younger: when I grow up I'm going to be a snowboarder. How did I come to this conclusion? Nobody knows. I grew up in the middle of Seattle, no one in my family did snow sports, and my only means of transportation was the public city bus. Once I started middle school they offered a winter snowboard programme. That's what opened the floodgates to a world I would soon call home. I would find rides to the mountains any way I could. I used to take the public bus holding all my snowboard gear to the outside of Seattle, just so I could catch a carpool to the mountain. I guess you could say I was determined. Eventually I came across Mt. Hood. If I wasn't hooked before, you could bet I was now. The magic of Mt. Hood, a place that holds so much beauty and snowboard history. Every time I see this mountain, it steals my heart. That's why I question if snowboarding is a sport. I see it as more of a lifestyle, a passion project. The gateway to a heart-fulfilled life.

This path is not an easy one, it comes with many physical and mental breakdowns. It's when you break through that and you see the positive impact your hard work has on others. I feel a shift in the social consciousness of the snowboard industry, I'm seeing a lot more girls being given a lot more opportunities. I also think it could be our downfall, I don't want to be given anything. I want to work hard, earn it, and own it. And after that I want to continue to grow and inspire others to do the same. It's not the time to wait and be given an opportunity, it's the time to take it.

Naima Antolin

TANON GIRLS

ELENA WATERFALL
(RÉVÉ FRAIS 28C)

BANDES   F8   25s   50s -> GRIS

BANDES   F11   15s   25s -> CONTRASTE OK
BANDE   F8   #12s   FILTRE 4 1/2 ->

(RÉVÉ 24°C)   -
BANDES   F11   FILTRE 4 1/2   32 SEC   ~~48 SEC~~
            50 SEC   ~~45 SEC~~

⚠ BANDELETTES TEST 30X40 ROULÉES PAR
K.CK-ABS PRINCESS

FEUILLE1   F11   Fi 4 1/2   45 SEC
    TEMPS RÉVÉ +/- 10 MIN

FEUILLE 2   F11   Fn 4   52 SEC

TANON GIRLS

P67 ZOOM RATIOS

MANIFAX 4

OBJO 105mm : MAXI 60/69 mm

OBJO 80 mm : MAXI 42/69 mm

OBJO 75 mm : MAXI 40/69 mm

BLEACH
FARMER MOERSCH

EN LOCAL : SUPER GALÈRE, À ÉVITER, BAVE
PARTOUT, BRULE LES CLAIRS.
    1 BOUCHON DANS 500 ML.

EN FEUILLE : 3 BOUCHONS DANS 2L. 24°C.
30 SEC => FIX => 30 SEC => F.X.

    CLAIRS BRÛLÉS 100%.
    MEDIUM LÉGÈREMENT + CLAIRS
    NOIRS INTACTES

TEINTE SIMILAIRE.

CHRISTY CRUISING

3ème FEUILLE SÉANCE

70 SEC F11   FILTRO 5
+ VIGNETTAGE

-> PARFAIT

PS ASEZ RÉVÉ : MARQUES

STYLO NOIR
STYLO NOIR
CRAYON

DÉSIRÉE STALEFISH

PAS DE
VIEUX
BRUN
DISPO

F16   GRADE 5   20 SEC
+ VIGNETTAGE   20 SEC

FEUILLE N°1   N° SÉANCE : 1

BORDURE : SANS FILTRE, F16, SANS
            PASSE-NEGA , VITRE : 5 SEC
TON GRIS
=> MANQUE CONTRASTE   + BORDURE DSP. TROP FONCÉE

    FEUILLE 2 :
20 SEC   F 5.6   FILTRE N°5
    BORDURE 6 SEC   LÉGER VIGNETTAGE
                    15 SEC

FEUILLE SÉANCE : N° 2

    GOOD!

ARTISTIC PROCESS

Shooting action sports with a medium format Pentax 6x7 – fixed lens, manual focus, ten photos per film roll – is a pretty stupid challenge of its own, but the quality and depth of field is magnificent. Etching, scratching, painting, bleaching my favourite negatives of the following series is also an absurd feeling, but it's a statement. I'm ready to destroy my most precious negatives to bring out more personality, more texture, more words. Lith printing is an old-school darkroom process is and it's a nightmare to control.

The payback is a highly contrasted photograph, with texture and pepper marks, natural sepia and beautiful tones. Because the only paper which gives me this result has been out of production for many years, the last remaining stock of sheets is a treasure to me. No test sheets, each one had to be good. Combining all my experiences in analogue photography, copperplate etching and darkroom printing, from start to finish, this process is an absolute make-it-count, all-or-nothing commitment to the art.

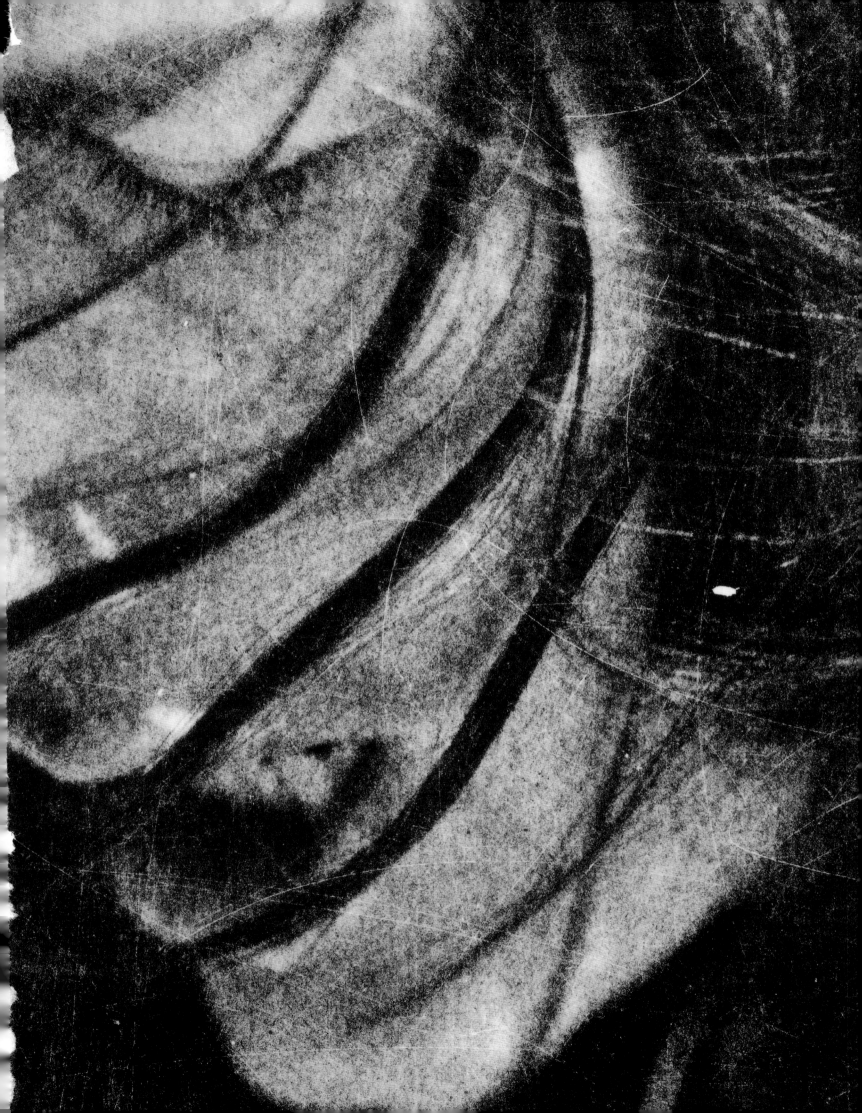

AIGHT BITCH

Drypoint etching on negative
Silver-gelatin lith print
Jérôme Tanon
40x50 cm - 2020

Elena Graglia & Alieke Hoi
Helsinki, Finland

LET'S GET IT BITCH

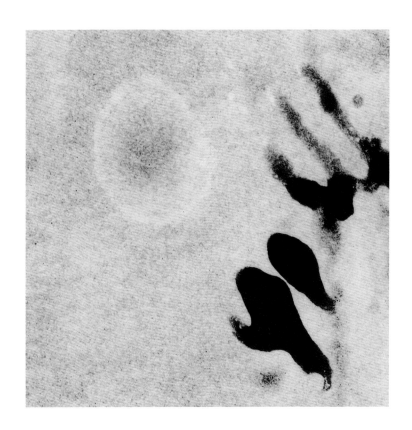

WATERFALL

Potassium ferricyanide on negative
Silver-gelatin lith print
Jérôme Tanon
40x50 cm - 2019

Elena Graglia
Helsinki, Finland

KICK-ASS PRINCESS

Drypoint etching on negative
Silver-gelatin lith print
Jérôme Tanon
40x50 cm - 2019

Silje Norendal
Flachauwinkl, Austria

VAIL GANG

Silver-gelatin lith print
Jérôme Tanon
40x50 cm - 2020

Kailey Bogart, Gidget Holden, Olivi Lisle,
Ashley Bogart & Viviana Oram
Ms. Superpark 2020
Eldora, CO, USA

FUTURE

Sharpie on negative
Silver-gelatin lith print
Jérôme Tanon
40x50 cm - 2019

Zoi Sadowski-Synnott
Flachauwinkl, Austria

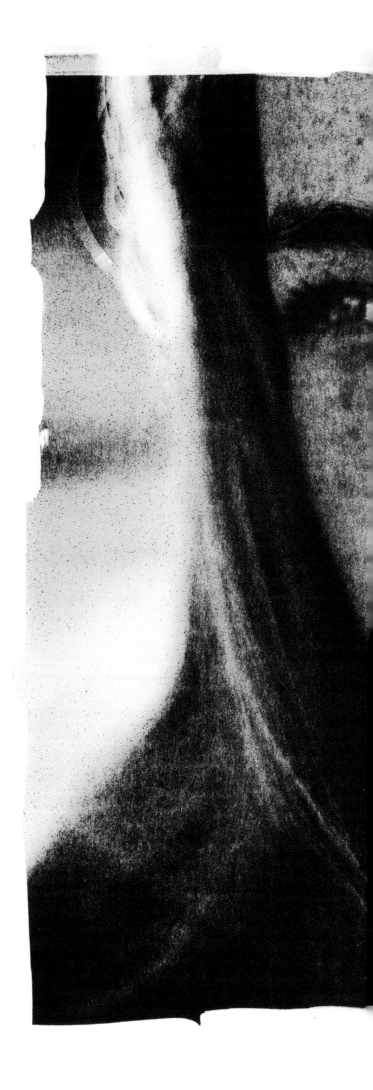

FUTURE

NOTE TO SELF

Drypoint etching & Posca on negative
Silver-gelatin lith print
Jérôme Tanon
40x50 cm - 2020

Ylfa Rúnarsdóttir
Ms. Superpark 2020
Eldora, CO, USA

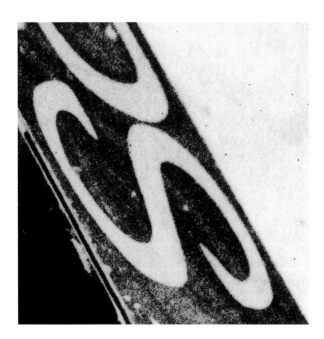

FUCK THAT HURT

Drypoint etching & Sharpie® on negative
Silver-gelatin lith print
Jérôme Tanon
40x50 cm - 2020

Elena Graglia (hurt) & Enni Rukajärvi
Helsinki, Finland

THAT HURT

OF MY SEASON ?

DESIREE STALEFISH

Box cutter & tape on negative
Silver-gelatin lith print
Jérôme Tanon
40x50 cm - 2020

Desiree Melancon
Ms. Superpark 2020
Eldora, CO, USA

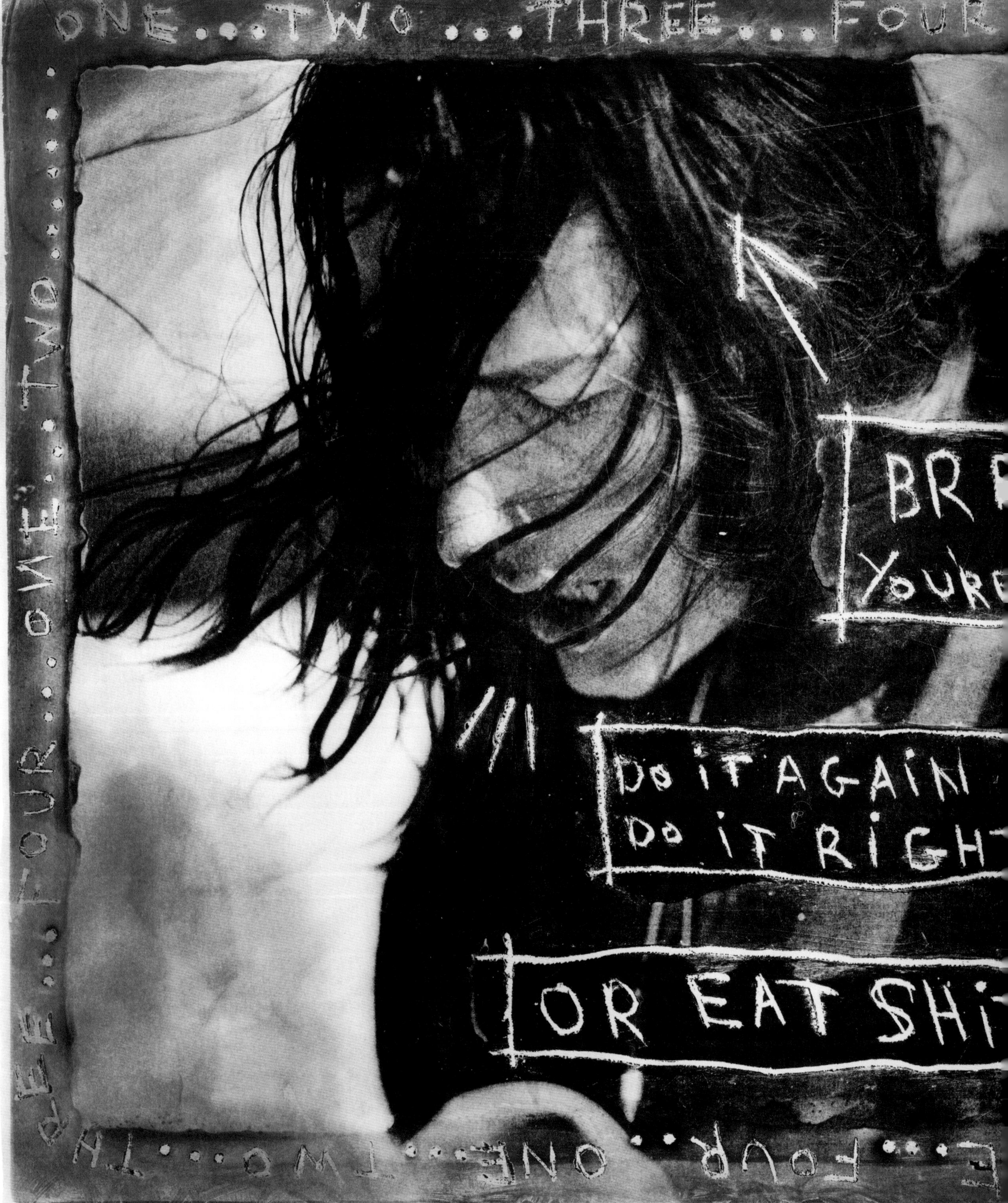
ONE...TWO...THREE...FOUR
BR
YOU'RE
DO IT AGAIN
DO IT RIGHT
OR EAT SHI

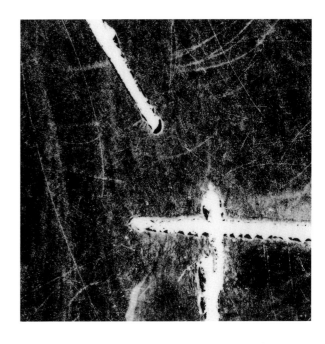

BREATHE

Drypoint etching, lithographic ink & potassium ferricyanide on negative
Silver-gelatin lith print
Jérôme Tanon
40x50 cm - 2020

Desiree Melancon
Eldora, CO, USA

METHOD GIRL

Drypoint, sandpaper etching & lithographic ink on negative
Silver-gelatin lith print
Jérôme Tanon
40x50 cm - 2020

Christy Prior
Ms. Superpark 2020
Eldora, CO, USA

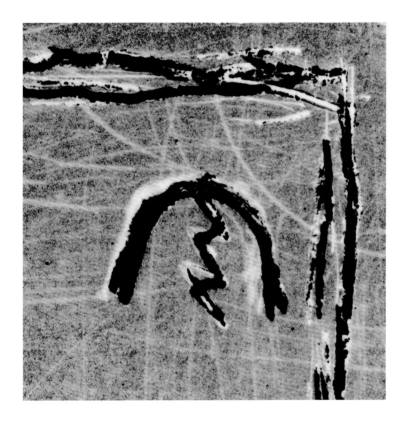

NIRVANA

Drypoint, sandpaper etching & lithographic ink on negative
Silver-gelatin lith print
Jérôme Tanon
40x50 cm - 2020

Nirvana Ortanez
Quebec City, Canada

NiRVANA

THINK ABOUT NOTHING ...
Welcome
All Visitors
Please Sign
in at Office
Entrance on
Lower Level
DON'T
FUCK UP
D.M.

ROOF DROP TO KINK

Drypoint etching, Posca & potassium ferricyanide on negative
Silver-gelatin lith print
Jérôme Tanon
40x50 cm - 2020

Desiree Melancon
Eldora, CO, USA

ALEXIS

Silver-gelatin lith print
Jérôme Tanon
40x50 cm - 2020

Alexis Roland
Ms. Superpark 2020
Eldora, CO, USA

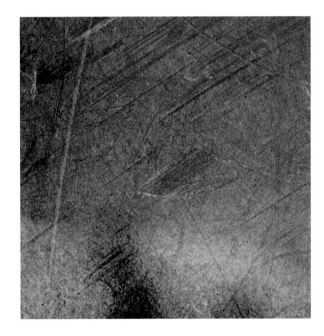

YLFA'S

Sandpaper etching & lithographic ink on negative
Silver-gelatin lith print
Jérôme Tanon
40x50 cm - 2020

Ylfa Rúnarsdóttir
Helsinki, Finland

KING

Drypoint etching & lithographic ink on negative
Silver-gelatin lith print
Jérôme Tanon
40x50 cm - 2020

Marie-France Roy
Whistler BC, Canada

KING

NAIMA ANTOLIN

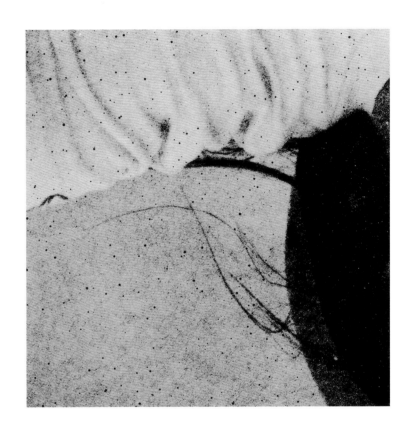

NAIMA ANTOLIN

Drypoint etching & Posca on negative
Silver-gelatin lith print
Jérôme Tanon
40x50 cm - 2020

Naima Antolin
Ms. Superpark 2020
Eldora CO, USA

BALDFACE

Silver-gelatin lith print
Jérôme Tanon
40x50 cm - 2020

Estelle Pensiero & Robin Van Gyn
Baldface lodge
Nelson BC, Canada

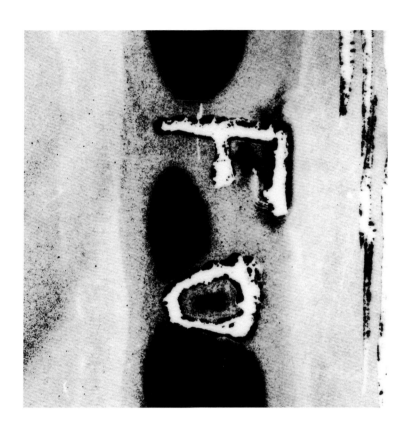

ROBIN & ESTELLE

Drypoint etching, lithographic ink & potassium ferricyanide on negative
Silver-gelatin lith print
Jérôme Tanon
40x50 cm - 2020

Robin Van Gyn and Estelle Pensiero
Baldface Lodge, Canada

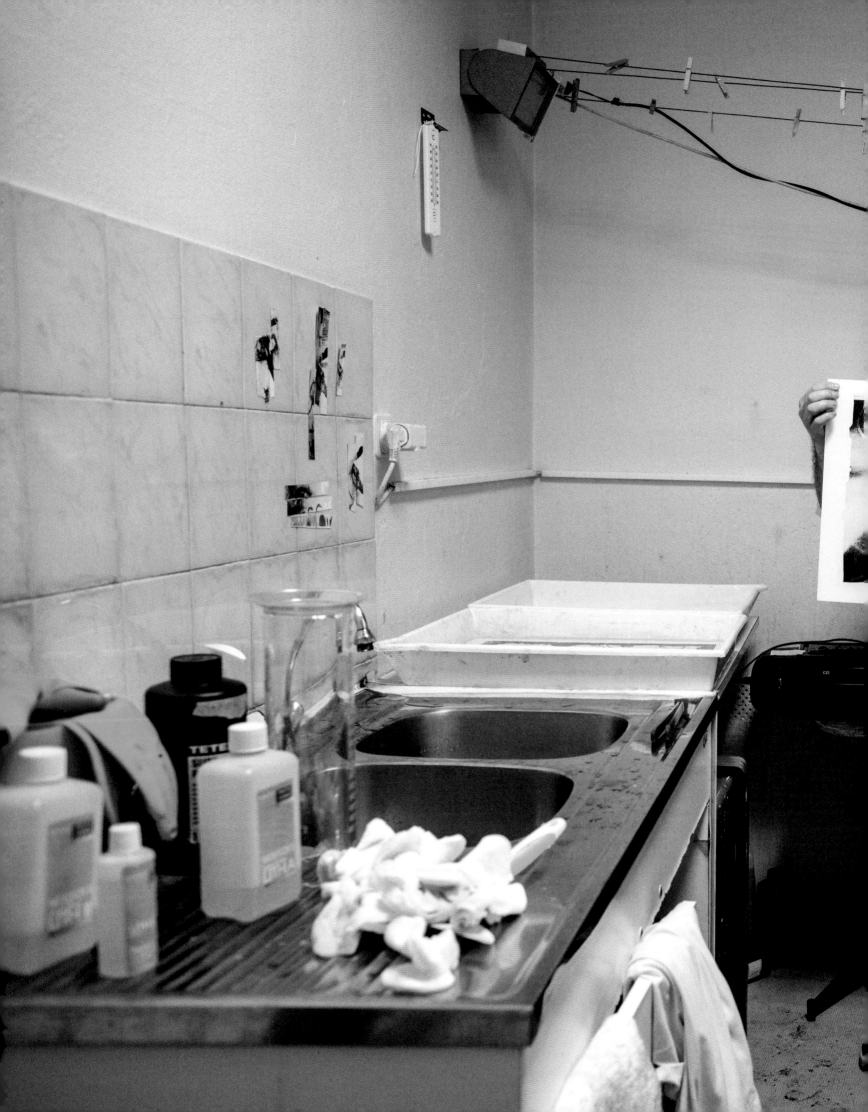

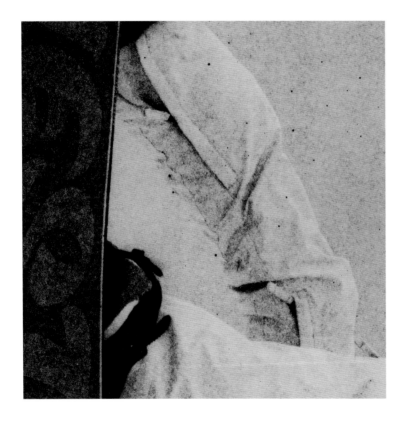

BAD KID

Potassium ferricyanide & fineliner on negative
Silver-gelatin lith print
Jérôme Tanon
40x50 cm - 2020

Elena Könz
Laax, Switzerland

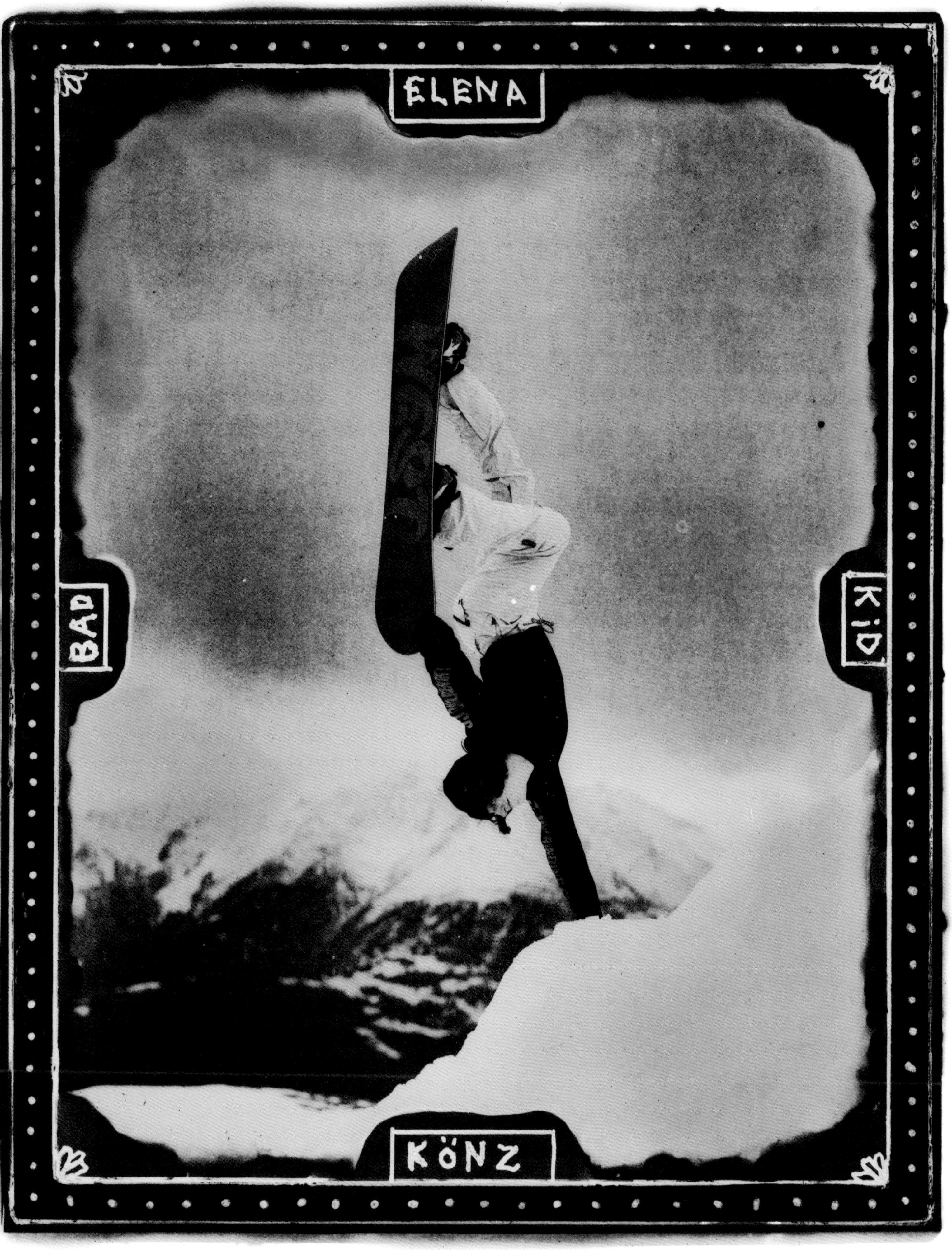
ELENA
BAD
KID
KÖNZ

FUCK TRUMP

Drypoint etching on negative
Silver-gelatin lith print
Jérôme Tanon
40x50 cm - 2020

Desiree Melancon
Eldora, CO, USA

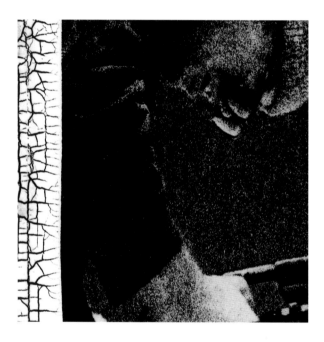

5-0 BALLS

Posca on negative
Silver-gelatin lith print
Jérôme Tanon
40x50 cm - 2020

Desiree Melancon
Kemmerer, WY, USA

WHISTLER SLED GANG

Silver-gelatin lith print
Jérôme Tanon
40x50 cm - 2020

Marie-France Roy, Leanne Pelosi
& Robin Van Gyn
Whistler BC, Canada

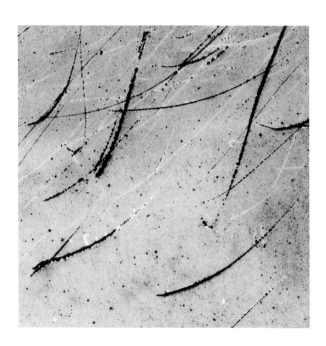

CHRISTY CRUISING

Sandpaper etching on negative
Silver-gelatin lith print
Jérôme Tanon
40x50 cm - 2020

Christy Prior
Ms. Superpark 2020
Eldora CO, USA

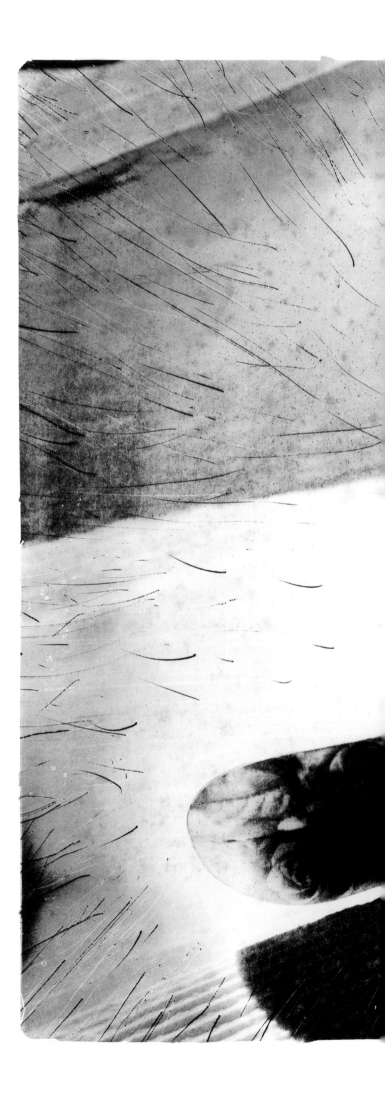

FREEDOM

Drypoint etching & electrical tape on negative
Silver-gelatin lith print
Jérôme Tanon
40x50 cm - 2020

Elena Könz
Laax, Switzerland

FREEDOM

ANNA SWITCH INRUN

Silver-gelatin lith print
Jérôme Tanon
40x50 cm - 2020

Anna Gasser
Audi Nines 2019
Oetztal, Austria

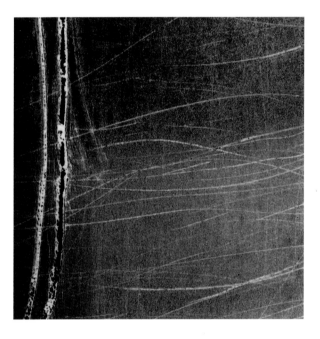

ANNA

Drypoint, sandpaper & lithographic ink on negative
Silver-gelatin lith print
Jérôme Tanon
40x50 cm - 2020

Anna Gasser
Flachauwinkl, Austria

ELENA NOSESLIDE INDY

Drypoint etching on negative
Silver-gelatin lith print
Jérôme Tanon
40x50 cm - 2019

Elena Graglia
Helsinki, Finland

ELENA

BANDE DE TROUS D'UCS

In English: 'Peace out assholes'
Drypoint, sandpaper etching & lithographic ink on negative
Silver-gelatin lith print
Jérôme Tanon
40x50 cm - 2020

Marion Haerty
Chamonix, France

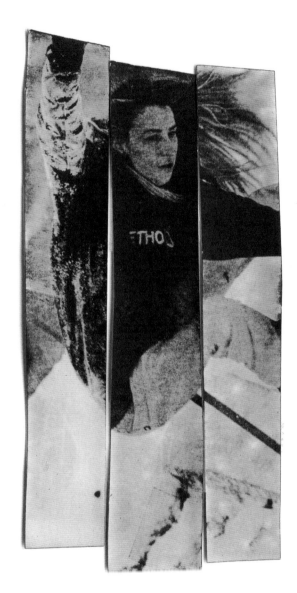

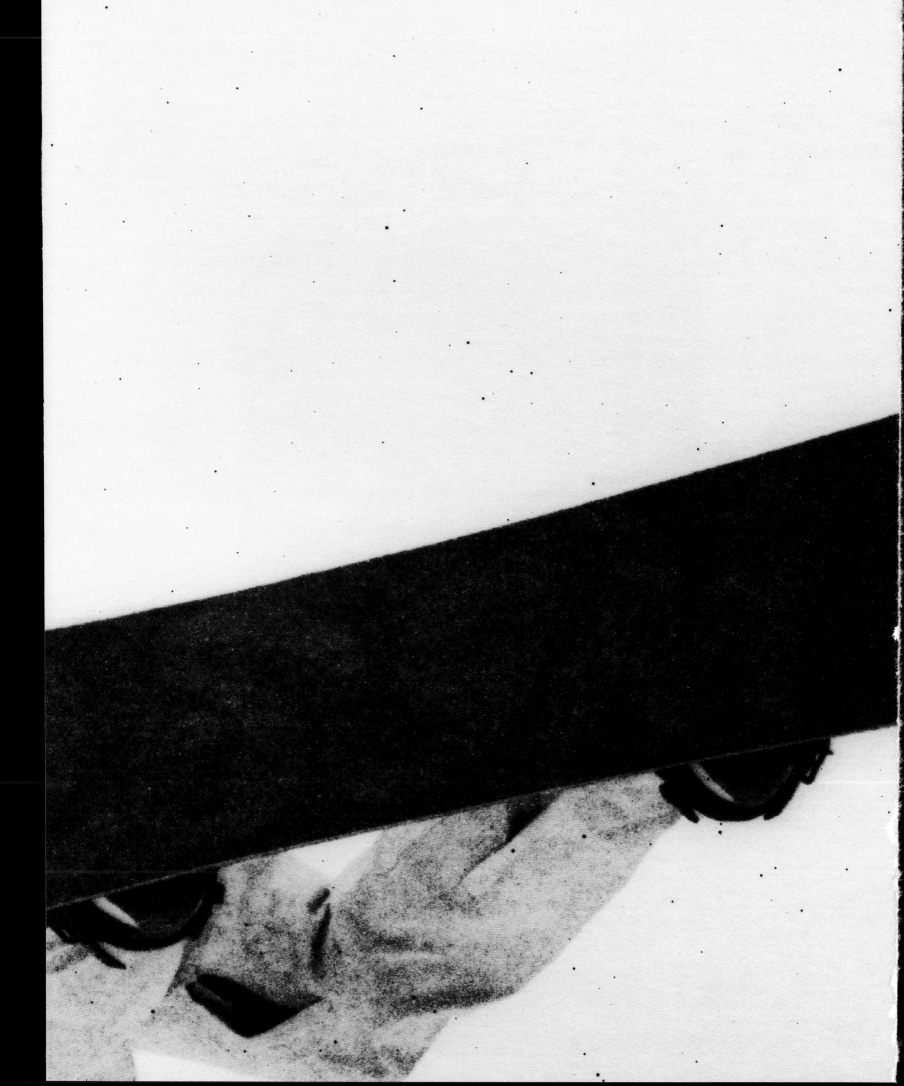

C R A F T I N G

Shooting.

With the Pentax 6x7 camera and 400 ISO BW films. I use mostly Ilford HP5+ and Kodak TMAX. I regularly push the films of one to three stops, up to 3200 ISO, to increase sensitivity, grain and contrast. The film rolls are normally developed after each trip, revealing the negatives.

Etching of the selected negative.

Etching is done on the gelatin side of the 6x7cm negative with drypoint, inks, markers, Posca, tape, sandpaper, pins and potassium ferricyanide solution. When using the gelatin as if it were a copper plate, after etching with a drypoint, the ink has to be laid on the negative then cleaned from the surface; this way the ink stays only in the etches. Any piece of text has to be written mirrored, from right to left.

Preparation of the lith developer bath.

The A and B lith solutions are mixed with warm water and a bit of old developer saved from the previous session. A few pages of smaller dimension need to be 'burned' to produce the crucial semiquinone molecules. This product of the reaction is also a catalyst of the same reaction. Because of that, lith developers are very unstable, hard to control and the infectious chain reaction will only provide the desired result for a few sheets. The more the solution is used, the more contrast, pepper effect, texture and warmer sepia tone, until it is exhausted.

Exposure of the paper.

From now on we are in the dark, or in the safety red. Contrast is not controlled by colour filters as in standard print making, but by the exposure time and developer chemicals. Many tiny strips of paper have to be tested to determine the correct exposure time, usually between 15 to 200 seconds. When the enlarger is turned on and the timer starts, the precise dance of the hands can start. Dodge and burn mechanisms are achieved by creating shadows onto the paper, with cardboard tools and silhouettes done with the hands. The longer a shadow stays over a zone, the brighter it will end up. But you can only see the results after developing the paper, so you're just going by experience and gut feeling.

Lith Development.

The exposed paper is dipped in the developer tank. The paper has to stay nicely underwater or oxidation marks will appear. Nothing happens for two to twenty minutes until, very slowly, a pale grey silhouette of the photo magically comes up. Then all of a sudden the chain reaction starts, the paper is 'lithing' and deep blacks spread on the most exposed parts of the paper, just like a virus would do. Contrary to standard BW process, development never stops. The sheet has to be snatched from the tray exactly when the exposure is a few seconds from perfect, because ten seconds later it might have turned entirely black. The precious sheet is dipped into a stop-bath of cold water as fast as possible to stop the reaction. Each paper/developer combo brings different results. The only way to achieve the contrast, tone, sepia and pepper marks which give so much character to this series is with the *Moersch Lith Universal* developer and the *Adox Fine Print Varo Classic FB*. This beautiful 250g fibre-based paper was produced in Eastern Europe until the fabrication was reduced over the years and finally stopped in 2012. Back then I bought all of the little stock that remained, and since then I haven't been able to find it anywhere. I had about 70 sheets of 40x50cm to produce the final prints of the 28 etched negatives.

Hand development.

In many cases, I don't fix the print right away and keep adding developer, by hand, in certain areas of the print where I want to keep the reaction going. On a glass, still under red light, I apply developer with sponges and tissues, then quickly move it around and clean it away. It gives me more control over the shadows, but it's a risky game to play as marks and cold grey tones will appear.

Fixing.

The paper is dipped in a fixing bath for two minutes, stabilizing the silver salts. The paper is now no longer sensitive to light. A well-fixed silver-gelatin print can last virtually forever.

Bleaching.

I put the print back on a sheet of glass to bleach areas with a solution of potassium ferricyanide, which I alternate with a solution from the fixing bath. Applied with a tissue and quickly moved around on the photo, this combo will brighten the highlights, erase the nice sepia tones and make star-like marks, so I only use it in a last resort scenario, and to clean the many marks appearing on the white borders.

Praying and cursing.

By then I have probably cursed 200 times and prayed too. The slightest mistake at any point of the process will ruin a print. Back hurts. You're breathing nasty chemicals all day and haven't left your 3 cubic metre isolated dark room. Suddenly it's 2:00 in the morning. You lose track of time. You are hungry AF. You can't use more than three sheets per negative because there is just no more of this specific photo paper left in the whole damn world. You had better make it count. It takes up to six hours of work to get your final result for just one negative, and even then you are rarely happy. It could always be better, but you've just got to let go and accept it, as if it was your own child.

Cleaning.

The finished print is cleaned from any chemicals in running water for at least an hour. It is then gently drained on a sheet of glass and hung to dry slowly for 24 hrs.

Flattening.

A dry print will curl a lot on the sides and corners, so a hot-press must be used to counter this effect and make them nice and flat for storing or framing.

EK

As a kid I used to sit in front of my window drawing pictures of the Engadin mountains; the same mountains where I later found my love of snowboarding. Drawing and snowboarding were the two hobbies that meant the most to me when I was growing up. However, for a long time the two passions remained separate worlds. Often in life I was told what was right and what was wrong, how I should be and how I should act. That I should stop snowboarding and do more art, or that I was behaving 'like a boy'.

I'm lucky that by rebelling against this pressure I found places where the pursuit of unique style is valued and even promoted. I simultaneously had the chance to meet numerous brave and interesting people who inspired me to become what felt right. After years pursuing the two passions, I am starting to see more and more similarities between them. For both, it is about the creation of movement, resulting in forms which give each human a unique style, independent of gender and background

Elena Könz

Crystal Legoffe & Micah Anderson

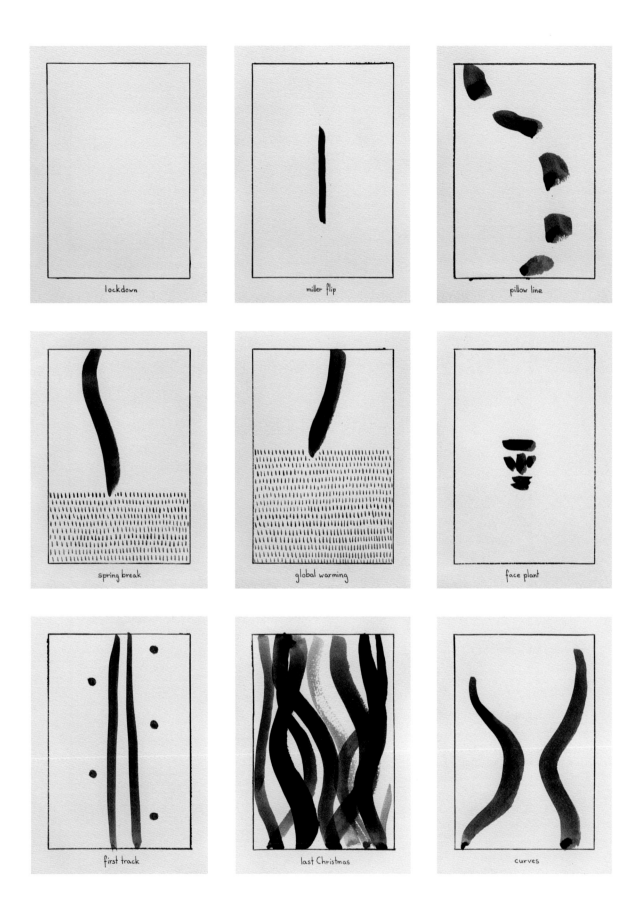

Elena Könz, *Studies of the line III*
Charcoal ink and snow on paper 14.8 x 21 cm

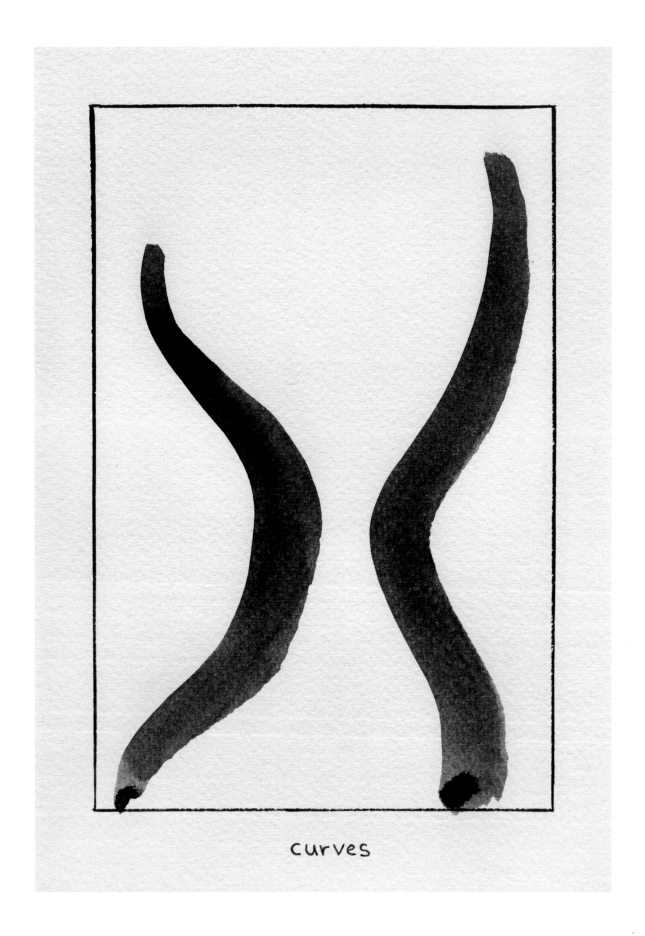

curves

Elena Könz, *Studies of the line III*
Charcoal ink and snow on paper 14.8 x 21 cm

Robin Van Gyn & Estelle Pensiero.

RVG

'What am I doing?', is the phrase that runs through my head, sometimes out loud, almost every time I stand at the top of a mountain. Hands are sweaty, tip toeing with a case of the shakes, a rather large crease carves deeper between my eyebrows. We make it look like it's no big deal on camera, but the fear is real.

Fear is the essential part, or else we would be like everyone else. It's what separates us, the drive or curiosity to cross a threshold that makes us something different. It's always there in anything and everything we do on small scales and large. Fear is the sign that lets me know I am crossing the boundary to something extraordinary, pushing my limits. This will be epic, or really fucking bad, but either way, I will go. I will cling to the mountain with my fingernails, I will check my set up at least three times, I will breathe, maybe yell, I will question everything. I will tighten my bindings again, punch my legs, I will say 'dropping in five', take another twenty, and then another thirty. But then the decision to go comes and you finally drop. Somehow, going down feels easy, you know this one, you've done it before... many times, it feels good, too damn good. It's so much ecstasy you forget about all that other sketchy stuff you did two minutes earlier. Before you even get a chance to recover, you're already planning your next line.

Robin Van Gyn

Estelle Pensiero & Robin Van Gyn

Robin Van Gyn

H.EDDY

AG

Live in the moment! That's a good approach to living your life in general, but it also describes best what I'm living for. When I'm snowboarding, that present moment is when I'm dropping in to hit a jump and all my thoughts are blown away. I am purely focused on this split second. I have to be, as it could very quickly go wrong if my mindset wasn't focused.

Since I started snowboarding it is these moments which have always been very special to me. These made me addicted. It simply captivated me that you are living so much in that present moment that you manage to fade out everything else. No other thoughts, no worries, no stress, no pressure – it's all gone while dropping in. Nothing comes close to that feeling.

I found freedom in snowboarding. With snowboarding I found something I can do my way. There is no set path and you can achieve your goals with determination and focus. And determination and focus are what I always had. I'm not giving up, I'm trying until it works.

Some find purpose early in life, some later. For me, snowboarding is my purpose and I am hoping to continue to inspire many other girls to achieve their dreams as I did, and still do.

Anna Gasser

Anna Gasser

LP

You are the only thing stopping yourself from kicking down the doors to create your own reality. I learned this lesson in my university days. My intentions were to become a professional soccer player and it all came to an abrupt halt...

I got into this car accident on the highway. My dreams were cut short. We were driving home from snowboarding and the driver fell asleep at the wheel. Miraculously, despite no seat belts or proper chairs for that matter... the eight people in the van clung on for dear life. I vividly remember flying through the air in the van and realizing this is NOT how I envisioned it all ending. My brother and my closest friends in the van... we hit a pole, shattered bones, crumpled metal. It was a bloody mess, to say the least. In the events that ensued, I was kicked off the junior national team, lost my status as I was 'focusing on another sport'... and realised that structured sport wasn't even giving me the time of day. Against my parent's wishes, I skipped finishing my second degree in engineering and made the move to Whistler with no plan, other than friends telling me that it'll be the best decision I would ever make in life. They were right – the mountains offered a place where you don't need anyone's approval to be happy. And that one-year hiatus from school turned into seventeen years and never going back! Moral of the story? When one door closes, another opens. Don't listen to your dad when he tells you you're going to become an engineer. Follow your heart. Always.

Leanne Pelosi

Leanne Pelosi

Jessa Gilbert, *Baldface Outback*
Acrylic on Canvas, 30" x 40"

Jessa Gilbert, *Macbeth Icefield, Kootenays*
Acrylic on Wood Panel, 18" x 24"

J G

Snowboarding has given me more than an activity to pass the time, it has given me freedom of movement and a vehicle to create artwork. I started snowboarding in New York State when I was ten and spent my youth battling it out with the boys in rail jams and slopestyle competitions since we often didn't have a women's category. Growing up with three brothers, I was used to fighting for a seat at the table and was elated to see female representation slowly growing through my high school and university years. I was fearless, untrained and only understood 'go bigger and try harder'.

I crashed a lot and wound up needing my fifth knee surgery by the time I was twenty-five, this time a full knee reconstruction. I was told by that surgeon I would never snowboard again, and should invest in more passive playtime after recovery. That knee surgery changed my life and shone a light on my love for snowboarding and the identity I had spent the last fifteen years carving out.

That following winter I tentatively stepped out on a splitboard in my new home of British Columbia out of sheer stubbornness and longing for reconnecting with snowboarding. I had a backpack full of art supplies and told myself I'd keep my board on the ground and delicately move through the mountains, so as to not further damage my new knee. The terrain I was able to access in BC, even with my weak, atrophied leg, left me in awe. I found myself being drawn into the process of creating artwork within that terrain with the same tenacity that I had when approaching a starting gate for a slopestyle competition. Skinning uphill with my splitboard naturally strengthened my legs and the further I pushed out, the more I felt home, both within my body and my painting practice.

I don't know who I would be without snowboarding, or what I would be creating without splitboarding opening my eyes to the beauty and awe-inspiring quality of the backcountry. The snowboard has taught me about perseverance and continues to teach me about sharing joy and the love for a day in the mountains, untouched powder, and new objectives beyond the lift line.

Jessa Gilbert

Silje Norendal

Crystal Legoffe

H. EDDY

ZSS

My parents packed me and my four siblings up to move from the northern beaches of Australia to the Southern Alps of New Zealand when I was six years old. Mum and Dad were both keen skiers growing up, however, Dad had broken all the bones in his left foot in an accident and was unable to wear a ski boot and ski for quite a few years. Missing the snow, he headed to Whistler to learn to snowboard and met Mum there, so the snow had always held a special place in their hearts.

Growing up, I was my two older brothers' biggest fan; it didn't matter what they were doing, I wanted to do the same. I remember the first time I skateboarded and dropped in on a skate ramp. I was seven years old and determined that if my brothers could do it, I could do it. I got rolled from what I can remember, but I tried again until I got it. I was ripping around on a skateboard for a while until I took my first snowboard lesson at Snow Park, New Zealand with my sister Reilly who asked me to join her. My brothers were already ripping around on their snowboards and thought the park was one of the best places in the world... From that day, I was hooked. It was like skateboarding in one of my favourite places, in the mountains and on the snow.

Snow Park was a resort on top of one of the town's surrounding ranges dedicated to having as many park features in one space as possible. My mum saw that the place was struggling to make a profit so she started taking care of it to keep it alive. My family lived up the mountain during those seasons, which in New Zealand is a crazy thing to do, most resorts are at least a 30-45 minute drive from the nearest town. I feel like I had a good early experience of what snowboarding was all about. I would get to watch the pros that would come from overseas for our three-month season, as well as the local frothers that would come up every single weekend and take cheeky days off work to make the most of the snow while we had it. When I look back at the Snow Park days, that's when I fell in love with snowboarding, the mountains and the community that surrounds it. The place heart-breakingly closed down in 2012 when the money ran dry. I kept snowboarding, though, and my parents supported me to join a local programme at Cardrona where I could get coached with other snowboarders my age. I was fourteen when I did my first stint overseas and have been doing back-to-back winters ever since.

Snowboarding, for me, is what I love to do most. Whether it's riding the park, hitting jumps and rails or riding pow in the backcountry. I love it all and I always love pushing myself to learn new tricks. And although over the years I have spent a lot of time riding with the boys, it has been amazing to ride with some of the best female riders in the world; I think we push each other, and I think it shows. But at the same time, we are all really supportive of each other. I will never forget when I had finished my run at one of my first comps, a World Cup Big Air in Copper Mountain, Colorado, and I was standing at the bottom by myself and Jamie Anderson came over and gave me a big hug. The progression we have seen in women's snowboarding has been insane. I feel privileged to be part of it and I hope I can be a part of that for many years to come.

Zoi Sadowski-Synnott

Zoi Sadowski-Synnott

Eatin bags of dicks

Margot Rozies AKA Missa, *Candy time*
Ballpen and fineliner

KM

I grew up in a small mountain town in Slovakia. I started snowboarding at the age of ten at a local ski resort where my parents had a buffet/bar. They were too busy running the business so they would give free beer and shots to any friend who would take me snowboarding and 'look after me'. I never had to buy a season pass because the chairlift operators would also get free drinks at my parents' bar.

For the first four years I mostly rode powder or went freeriding with local pioneers. They were real assholes and never waited for me even though they saw I could not snowboard very well. I was the only girl in the group and had to keep up. It was a good challenge. During this time, I also used to snowboard a lot with my dad. Fear wasn't really in my dictionary so I had a lot of nasty-looking falls. How it's possible that I have never broken a single bone in my body is beyond me.

Everyone remembers me as the little girl in a Slipknot hoodie wearing a motocross helmet so I did not crack my skull the fuck open. Ironically, my first competition's name was Lords of Metal and I was so nervous when thinking about it that I puked the night before. My beginnings as a competitive snowboarder in Slovakia were funny. At least four girls had to sign up for women's competition to open. Often there were less than four of us so you couldn't really be 1st, 2nd or 3rd. You just did your tricks and had fun. The competition was only for the boys and I joined in anyway.

My first real competition was in New Zealand, where I got to know girls who are real 'sick' snowboarders. I never really cared about the competition result unless I was happy with my riding and runs. What I gained from this experience was seeing what other girls can do. This inspired and pushed me to also try to become a girl who can do these sick tricks too. I am very grateful for these girls, the friendships and the community. I am excited to see where women's snowboarding is going. Girls, the future looks good.

Klaudia Medlova

Lia-Mara Bosch

Desiree Melancon

Eivy, Stend Tallshop. The Int...

Flux Bindings
...lab Brand
...al Headwear
ROLLHAUGE...

Amanda Maccaro

GOOFY AKA Yung Pantz

...urton, Anon Opt.

Alexa McCarty
REGS
- CAPITA
- UNION
- HOWL

:)

Micah Anders...
Goofy...

Roxy Nitr...
Oakley Uni...
Blackstra...
...ich LSP

...mashley
Giangregorio
...mashley-gian

...tance:
GOOFY

NITRO-
·THE NORTH-
FACE

...OR DIE IND.

...TIM... ...AHOUTS

Christine Savage
Regular

Burton, Native Eyewe...
Driscollway...

AMANDA
HANKISO...

GOOFY

...IMA
...NTOLIN   Reg.

Kristin Jessen
Reg.

The Interior Plain Project
Damage Boardshop
...Blaster

Christ...

Goofy...

Melissa Riitano :)

GOOFY
K2
O'NEILL
DANG!
CRAB G...
BCA
BRIGHTON...

CRYSTAL LEGOFFE
GOOFY
YES SNOWBOARDS
YUKI THREADS
BASIC
ELECTRIC

Veronigi
Hanssen
Regular
NICHE snowboards
PROTEST sportswear

V/T
L1

Nora Beck, Jenna Kuklinski, Christine Savage, Nelly Steinhoff, Sadie Maeda, Mary Walsh, Kaleah Opal, Nirvana Ortanez, Micah Anderson, Savannah Golden, & Melissa Riitano. Superpark 2020.

Alexis Roland & Kaleah Opal

AR

It's crazy because snowboarding is such a mental sport. For me, snowboarding is a love-hate relationship where the biggest struggle is my own fears. I love it more than anything, but if my fears can take hold of me, it sours the relationship to the point where it's unrecognisable and only causes pain.

There was one day about five years ago when I decided I wasn't going to let my fear control me anymore. I still remember it clearly, my coach wanted me to try a new trick that day, a hard-way back 180 on. I was terrified, I didn't want to do it. So I did what I often did, I gave it the type of try where you make it look like you are going for the trick, but aren't actually committing or trying to land it. After about ten tries I was frustrated. I was too scared to commit because I didn't want to get hurt.

As I sat at the top of the hill thinking about the trick, I kind of had a vision of my life. In that vision, there were two very distinct paths. On the one path, I would continue to half-ass my attempts of new tricks. I would never end up really getting better. In fact, I would probably get worse as time went on. This was the safe path. I wouldn't get hurt ... but my dreams and snowboarding career would likely fade away. On the other path, I would fully commit. I would fully commit to this trick and do everything in my power to actually try and land it, and I would do the same with every other trick. This was terrifying. I would have to face all my fears head-on, I wouldn't run from them. And I'd probably get hurt. Most of the time it probably wouldn't be bad, other times it would probably be brutal. But with that, the possibilities would be endless. I could see myself progressing and achieving my wildest dreams. After that vision, I knew what I had to do. The thing is, no matter what you do you will always have some struggle, fears, or pain that you have to deal with. Life is about choosing which pains you are ok with and what dreams are worth it. It's not easy by any means.

Five years ago, I accepted the struggles, pain, and fear that came with snowboarding. I decided snowboarding was worth struggling for. Ever since then, I have felt empowered to face my fears, and try that new trick or hit that sketchy spot. Yes, I might fall and get hurt, but the idea, the dream I am chasing is more important to me and it inspires me to give snowboarding my all. That one decision and the constant reaffirmation of that decision has freed me to do the most insane things, things that I would have never believed possible for me. Snowboarding has truly been a gift. I am so grateful for it and all the things I have learned from it. All I want to do is share it all and my passion for it with others.

Alexis Roland

Marion Haerty

AB

I grew up in Montreal and I started snowboarding in 1993 when I was in 8th grade. I was the only girl at school who snowboarded. The few guys who rode said I was a poser and didn't want me to ride with them.

So it was quite lonely at first as I didn't know anyone, but I loved it so much that I never cared. Snowboarding made me feel so free and confident. I fell and fell and fell but I was completely determined and addicted. I would find a ride one hour outside of Montreal to Mont St-Sauveur and would watch guys around the resort and copy their tricks to know what to do.

It changed my life so fast. I became so in love with the sport. I quit every other sport I did and dedicated all my time to saving money so I could move to Whistler and become the best I could be. I truly felt like this was my destiny. I met new amazing people every weekend and searched for events where I could compete. My dream was to be sponsored and travel the world because of snowboarding. I was fully tunnel vision and worked so hard to make it happen.

It's brought me the biggest highs and lows and it taught me to face my fears. From failures and injuries, I've learned my biggest lessons. What an amazing journey it has been, I've luckily been pro for almost twenty years. So that's a long time to meet incredible like-minded people, see the world and try new things... I am still fully addicted to snowboarding and can't wait for the snow to kiss the mountains every November and reunite with friends.

I have to thank snowboarding for changing my life and for showing me all these new possibilities that life has to offer.

Annie Boulanger

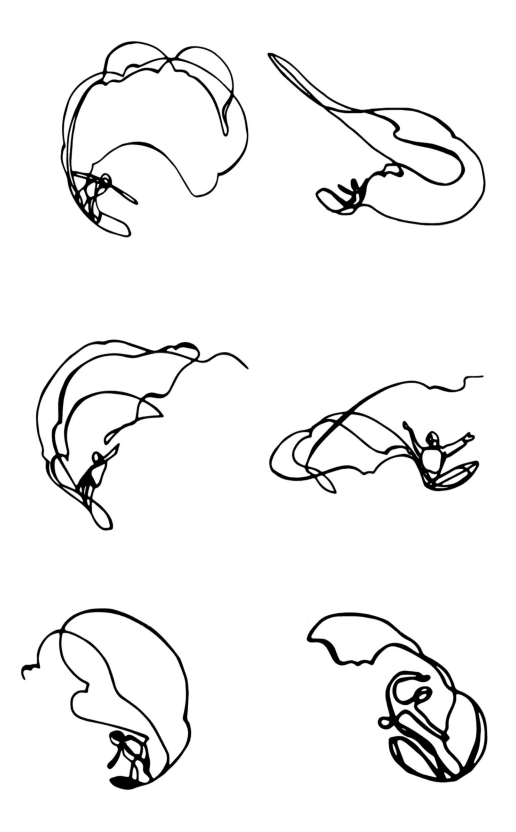

Annie Boulanger

MB

This sounds strange to write ... but I think me and snowboarding were just meant to happen. It fills most of my early memories and I really can't imagine my life without it. I don't think I could have avoided it; my mum and dad did many seasons and were definitely 'snowboarders', so it was almost natural that I would start riding at some point. I guess from about eighteen months old I was on a board. My dad even used to ride with me strapped to his chest before then.

Everything else has kind of just happened along the way. Luckily I've enjoyed it, and luckily I'm ok at it! I've also been super lucky to have had an amazing bunch of people around me over the years who only want to see me keep enjoying it, but also support me with whichever way I want to take it. I love competing, I love bashing pistes, slashing powder, I love being in the streets (especially after this years trip to Finland with dad in tow), I'm just so into snowboarding, what can I say!

A lot of my life so far has been spent living in our motorhome bouncing from resort to resort whilst juggling school work, but I'm ok with that. Snowboarding has meant that I've got to meet some amazing people and made some great friends, and also ridden with some impressive snowboarders like Gigi Ruf and Jenny Jones. I'm still waiting for the day I get to ride with Lucas Baume though, he's my favourite snowboarder by far, I just dig his style so hard!

There are still a lot of other things I'm into: skating, cycling, cats, music, pretty much most things a teenager is interested in I guess, but somehow it always comes back to snowboarding and I think that's my path, everything else is a bonus. Maybe when I'm a bit older and look back at it all, I'll think it's all pretty crazy – the things that have happened and the opportunities I've had, but I've never done anything I didn't want to and now I'm getting a bit stronger, wiser ... it feels like it's just kind of falling into place. Thank you snowboarding! And everyone in it :)

Mia Brookes

NR

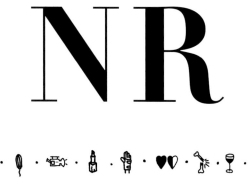

Snowboarding came into my life at twelve years of age after sabotaging a local downhill ski race, making sure I would not be selected to join the ski club in La Rosière. I strapped-in my snowboard to join a group called The Saturday Team, whose motto was to ride only for fun. We did everything, freestyle, freeride, we made little season edits. I had this pressure from my dad to 'succeed' and fit in the proper codes of society for a young lady. I loved snowboarding so much that I didn't want anyone to mess with it, let alone compete and feel even more pressure. In any case, my dad called it a misfit activity, and that was for the best. It was my free space, where I could express myself with no set goal. A space for creativity and sharing with others.

When I ride I feel wild, sensual and mighty. Snowboarding makes me discover a new side of my femininity, of the order of inner feelings. It helped me deconstruct the feminine codes that were not mine, and listen to my sensations.

Quite early I set off to explore the mountains through freeriding. At fifteen I was in a special class to learn how to be independent in the alpine. Freeriding has always felt like a synonym of free-will. Make your own choice, manage dangers and conditions to draw your own line. Up there I find my limits but also the strength to keep having fun. I also learned humility. It's an endless learning process. Understanding your environment is key to convey righteousness and respect.

When I started art school I understood the relation I had with snowboarding, as an artist. I made it the subject of my thesis: 'Her body resembled the letter S'. I find a sculptural relationship between the landscape we ride and the movement of riding. A relationship to the present moment. A cinematic relationship: pioneer dancer Isadora Duncan has widely inspired me. For her, wave mechanics is the founding principle, it is the observation of the movements of nature which inspire her dancing. Everything in nature is made of waves. It's about blending in the wave, creating a curve in harmony with nature. We fight gravity and let go at the same time, that is how movement is created. The dancer and the snowboarder are at the same time painter and actor on a gigantic canvas.

Natacha Rottier

Natacha Rottier, *Isadora's shoulder*
Mixed techniques of printing, ink, 21x27cm

Natacha Rottier, *My idol*
Mixed techniques of printing, ink, magazine paper, 21x27cm

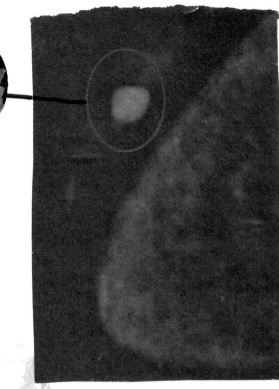

ÇARVE

G

GRAVITÉ

MOUILLÉE

SUSPENSION

ORBITE

SNOWSURFING

SENSUELLE

ONDULATION

ÇOURBE

PLAISIR

FLOWING

FLOTTER

SAUVAGE

JOUIR

SLASH

CARESSE

AIR

Natacha Rottier, *G-spot*
Marker pen, sticker letters, plastic bag, magazine paper, 21x27 cm

Veroniqi Hanssen

PRENDS - MOI

COULØIR REÇTILIGNE
RECTILIGNE

LA COMBE À JUSTIN

COULOIR RIVIERE GGGG GLIÈRE

LA GRANDE ÇASSE F.N
CASSE
ÇLASSE

Natacha Rottier, *Take-me*
Marker pen, sticker letters, acrylic, magazine paper, 21x27 cm

S C

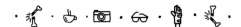

Growing up in Flims, one of the three mountain villages around the Laax resort, was a paradise. My family owns a little mountain hut next to a slope. My mum and my dad are both snow addicts. Every single minute they take me and my brother to the mountain to go skiing. My father tried snowboarding when I was five years old. Looking at how he did it fascinated me. My mum organised the gear, which wasn't easy at that time because snowboarding had only just come to Laax. My first few snowboard steps I learned together with my mum. We both learned it fast. After my first few turns, I knew – this is it! I love that shit.

As snowboarding wasn't popular at that time, I was by far the youngest snowboarder on the hill. With time I got better and faster and I loved it more and more. I skied sometimes – but not really – I was a snowboarder! The problem was that snowboarders weren't allowed to compete at the school race. In Flims every kid wants to be a ski racer. The teacher told my parents I would have to ski to enter the race, snowboarders are not allowed. My parents promised that it would be the last time I had to wear skis. I was unhappy and angry about that situation. Standing at the start gate – still angry – I went on and skied as fast as I could.

I won the ski race without too much of a surprise. The coach asked my father if I would like to join the racing team, they would take me as the youngest member. When my father turned to me, I reminded him of the promise: 'No, that was my last ski day!'

My grandfather, who hoped I would be a ski racer one day and follow my cousins' path, wasn't happy with my decision. Even now, after many good results, I don't know if he is proud of my snowboarding career. He died this spring so I won't be able to ask him anymore...

Sina Candrian

Ted Borland, Nirvana Ortanez, Justin 'Chip' Keniston,
Desiree Melancon, Justin Leveille, Mia Lambson, Pat Bridges

LB

· ⛰ · siɔk · 📱 · 🔥 · 🍾 ·

I started snowboarding because of my brother. Everything he was doing I had to try, so when I saw him snowboarding I did the same. I fell in love right away and since then I have never really stopped.

Being a girl in snowboarding when I was young wasn't too bad because I was at the snowpark every day. It's a small hill called Le Relais in Quebec, so everyone knew me and the boys were stoked to see a girl push herself. I still love going there today. It reminds me of so many fun memories riding with my friends from 12 pm to 10 pm.

I feel so lucky. I never thought I could be a pro snowboarder, for me snowboarding was just a passion. I started doing contests for fun aged thirteen and everything started from there. I always had fun competing and I think that's the most important thing. Snowboarding is a huge part of my life so I have had to make many sacrifices. Sometimes it's tough to not be home and be on the road for so long, not seeing your family and boyfriend, but I feel lucky to do what I do and it's worth the sacrifices.

Laurie Blouin

Laurie Blouin

HB

· ❀ · ◔◔ · ☠ · ♥♥ · ⛰ · ✿ · ☙ · 🍾 · ♘ ·

When I first began riding as a pro it was like a dream come true, but there were also some hard parts about this dream job for me at first. I remember tearing up and having a minor breakdown at an early team photoshoot. I didn't want to have my portrait taken and felt so uncomfortable in front of the camera. I could usually get away with making funny faces or pretending that I didn't care, acting tough covered up in shred gear, but when I had to look into a photographer's lens and just be 'ME', I felt awkward, ugly, out of place and unworthy. What I saw in photos of myself would shake my confidence. I didn't feel pretty enough, skinny enough. I'd pick apart all my shortcomings and imperfections, comparing myself to others and essentially crumbling the confidence I'd gained through the progress and accomplishments on my snowboard. It took some time to accept that this was also part of the job and to actually feel 'comfortable' in front of a camera. Over the years I've learned what to put energy into, and what to let go. Mainly, not to let fear and insecurities control how I live life. Life is too good! Almost two decades later and it's mostly good days and of course some not so good days. I don't let it get the best of me anymore but those self-depreciating, and critical thoughts can still creep in when I see a photo of myself.

It happened with this photo Jérôme took.

The difference now though, is after the flash of judgmental thoughts, I can take a breath and appreciate the hard work, crashes, scars, sun damage, laughter, sweat and tears that went into the person staring back at me. I'm kinder and more appreciative to that person because I understand all the imperfections, experiences and challenging parts of myself that have made my life's wild ride so amazing. Snowboarding has no doubt taught me a deeper and more valuable form of self-confidence, and photography has provided a mirror for self-reflection and forced me to reconcile with the 'ME' that I see in photos. It can be hard to love our genuine selves, especially as women, but it's become easier and I have snowboarding to thank for that.

Hana Beaman

"VALUE ADDED"

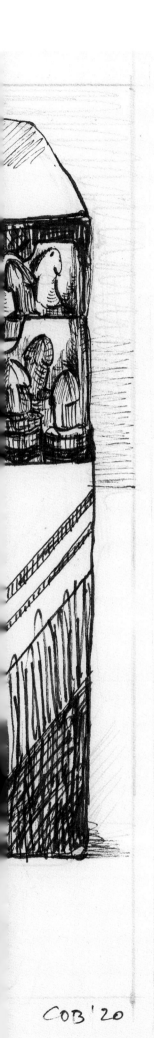

COB '20

Dude!

Mini-shred dude.

Triple-cork dude.

Lip-sliding rail dude.

Noam Chomsky quoting dude.

Open jacket crew dude, doubt fit dude,

socio-economically advantaged dude.

Trailer park dude, jock dude, rock dude.

64-pack of dude-alicious variety to press and

glide across a white canvas.

Oh, what?!

This box comes with a token sharpener?!

BONUS!

It's sharp. It shreds. It's heavier than it looks.

Makes blunt tips toned and dull edges honed.

Do all boxes come with one?

Nope, not yet.

But they should, and they will.

Nirvana Ortanez

NO

Family. For me, snowboarding happened because of my family. Growing up 150 miles from the nearest mountain, it's always been a wonder how I got into snowboarding. It started with the love and appreciation of the ocean and surfing. My dad was a significant influence with board sports throughout my life, and he got us all into snowboarding the minute my younger brother was old enough. Mom fell in love with it on our first trip up to Snow Summit, and after that we all became weekend warriors.

Back then there were always contests to participate in at the weekends in the local mountains whether it be a rail jam, slopestyle, or boardercross. Eventually my parents volunteered for USASA and our little family of four became part of the community. This community is what kept us coming back. Snowboarding at the root did, of course, bring us back too — learning new tricks, getting SoCal 'powders' — but looking back, the people we got to meet were sort of a hodgepodge, misfit family we got to see every weekend. It was something we all could do together, and the memories from it are forever.

I'm incredibly thankful for my family through it all, they were sending me to contests and supporting me even when finances were tough and sometimes unstable. I remember being told that 'I would never make it in snowboarding because we didn't have money', but that pessimism just made me want to pursue it even more. In contests, some people thrive and some people wane in the face of pressure — I was the latter towards the end. But, even though that path was winding down, I kept going, kept snowboarding and eventually I found a group of friends that made me realise that contests weren't the be-all and end-all.

With these friends you could film! You could make videos! You could learn how to pick up a camera, to edit, to put yourself out there for possible success or failure. Whatever the outcome, you at least added to the culture of snowboarding. I learned technical and creative skills that came with figuring out the alternative passage, and it opened up a whole new perspective on being a snowboarder.

Nirvana Ortanez

Nirvana Ortanez

MR

Snowboarding saved my life. Cheesy and said before, yes, but the truth is it really did.

I was a kid who was always bouncing off the walls and could never sit still. My parents decided that putting me in gymnastics would be a great fit for their monkey child and it was! Long story short, that led to me being a competitive gymnast and eventually getting injured and needing surgery. As I was getting back into the swing of it all, I realised that I had fallen out of love with the sport and decided to quit. From there I felt very lost, my identity had completely shifted, and the place I was living in didn't help much. It was a small town in Montana with not much to do if you didn't own a car to get out of town. There was no public transport, no skatepark, and no mountain nearby. I was thirteen at this point; kids my age were starting to smoke weed, drink, do pills, and other hard drugs like meth. It seemed normal at the time. But looking back that's a super fucked-up situation at that age. I was starting to go down a bad path of taking pills and just getting into stupid things. Thankfully never the really hard stuff.

Then I met my best friend Mariah. She snowboarded and I thought, wow that looks like so much fun. I'll never forget the first time I went, I pretty much fell on my face all day. But in the moments I wasn't falling I got that feeling of complete freedom. Shortly after, I got my very own snowboard and made friends on the mountain that felt more like family. We came from different places but were all bonded by this piece of wood under our feet. I finally felt like I had focus, a purpose, a place I belonged. I think it all kept me away from falling into a dark hole and some gnarly things like pills and harder drugs. Now I can't picture my life without snowboarding – the community of people involved are some of the most genuine and good-hearted people around. Snowboarding is where my mind can really be set free. Every movement is my own form of expression. It's easy to get lost in the process of doing a trick or turn with the exact style you want, or riding all day with your friends in clouds of powder just laughing. Life feels simple in those moments. I will forever be grateful for snowboarding.

Melissa Riitano

Melissa Riitano & Ylfa Rúnarsdóttir

FACE

to FACE

Elena Könz , *Face to face*
Gouache and gold leaf on paper

Melissa Riitano

Elena Graglia

EG

· 🧤 · 🖐 · ❀ · 👓 · 🎒 · 👑 · 💀 · ♥♡ ·

I was born in a small province in Northern Italy where the average person derives their happiness from the pursuit of material possessions such as cars and clothes. It always felt like I was out of context, an outsider. This discordance ultimately led me in the direction of mini ramp skateboarding and at seventeen my brother introduced me to snowboarding. The majority of my early years were spent hiking in the backcountry on the mountains close to my home-town, in the coveted Italian Alps. Knowing that I wanted to build my life around snowboarding, I became a snowboard instructor and fell in love with freestyle. After spending many years coaching, I decided to fully commit to realising my dream of becoming a professional snowboarder.

Following my departure from coaching life, at twenty-two I entered into a toxic relationship which challenged me for six years. It was a crazy, emotional roller coaster that lasted way too long and left me feeling completely drained, mostly because every day was spent arguing and fighting. The projection of his words was creating a deep anger inside myself and low self-esteem that obscured completely my bright side.

Little by little even snowboarding became overwhelming. Unable to focus on my own abilities and to experience that feeling of freedom that snowboarding gives you, I pretty much ended up filming him the whole time. In my time off from coaching, I was stuck there, with a camera in my hand and a spliff in the other one. Plus, I had to make it look like it was a pleasure for me, when of course it was not.

Eventually, I found myself compromising my dreams to the point of thinking that my future visions were just a childish fantasy or that I wasn't good enough. I was sad, hopeless and miserable. Not only was my relationship toxic, but I had also allowed myself to be surrounded by false friendships fuelled by codependency, addictions and alcohol.

The anxiety was growing up more and more until it was impossible for me to sleep or to go to work without crying. I felt that I was at the end. Which I was. But just at the end of that chapter.

When I decided to break up with him and to put myself in first place, I felt like I lost everything. Little did I know that the best times were yet to come. After all, it's never too late to change completely. From then on, I vowed to never again let anyone or anything hold me back from my full potential.

At the age of twenty-eight I embarked on a journey to prove to myself that I could make it on my own. Leveraging fear, self-doubt and lack of support in my favour, I was able to transmute them into motivation to achieve my goals of being unique, authentic and peaceful. I practised really hard, knowing that my talent would get me nowhere without commitment and dedication. I started to travel again, changed to a plant-based diet, explored human biodiversity in many countries, completed a yoga teacher training course in India and visited some of the best parks on the planet. My next big goal was to film a full part in the streets. But my experience was little and I wasn't involved with any film crews. Regardless, my friend Alieke and I decided to make it happen on our own. We reached out to a bunch of other girls from around Europe and organised a trip to Helsinki, where we all got shots and gained valuable experience in the streets. My hunger for snowboarding came back.

This past year, after blowing out 30 candles on my birthday cake, I was blessed with the opportunity to sign a few contracts which have been a huge help in making my video part a reality. I never thought that thanks to snowboarding I would meet my best friend, and my actual husband. My holistic vision for the future includes an abundance of opportunities to explore nature, building a farm with my husband and family, expanding my relationship with health and allowing my snowboarding to come full circle.

Elena Graglia

Elena Graglia

FORGET HOW MUCH
IT HURTS
AND TRY AGAIN

Tina Jeler, *Try again*
Handwriting

THANK YOU

This book would not exist without the tremendous support from the snowboard community. To the 350+ people who chipped-in for the crowdfunding: thank you! You made it happen.

A warm thank you to the snowboarders who trusted me with their very personal words. To the artists who got involved with heart and soul.

Special thanks to the following humans who put their hands in the mud to create this book with me: Matt Georges, Mary Walsh, Aurélien Leduc, Sophie & Theo Acworth, Jana Šmídová, James Smith and his team at ACC Art Books, especially Anna Emms, Craig Holden and Stephen Mackinlay.

Thank you Salomon Snowboards for supporting this project from the start.

Thank you SNOWBOARDER, Blue-Tomato, Ride Snowboards, Doodah, Burton Snowboards, Roxy, and Salomon Snowboards for supporting this book.

Thank you Absolut Park Flachauwinkl, Audi Nines Obergurgl, Laax, Whistler BC, Baldface lodge, Whitewater BC, Eldora CO for the help.

Thank you Siv Knudsen, Elena Könz, Linus von Moos, Leanne Pelosi, Jeff Keenan, Marie-France Roy, the Pensiero family, Robin Van Gyn, Ryan Kenny, Pat Bridges, Mia Lambson, Desiree Melancon, Justin 'Chip' Keniston, for the couches and drives along the road.

See you,
Jérôme

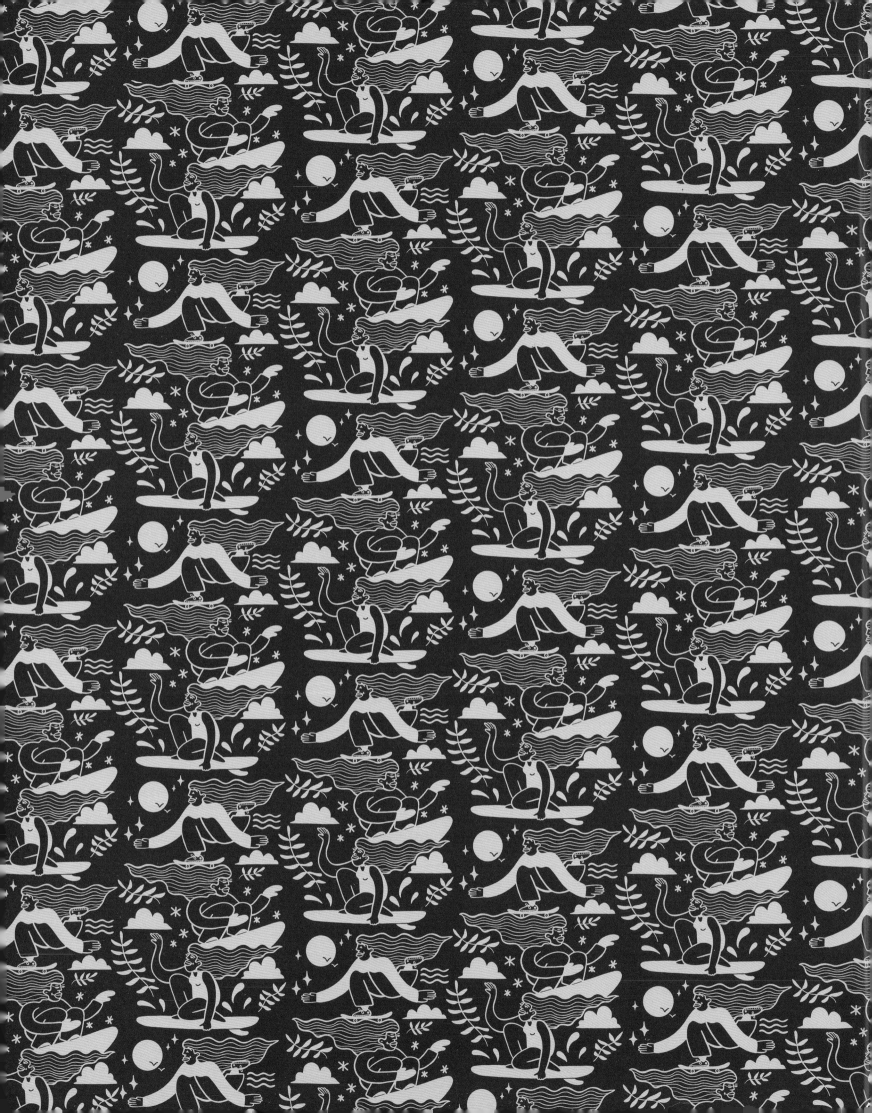